AYATOLLAH KHOMEINI

AYATOLLAH KHOMEINI

Matthew S. Gordon

N.Y.S.

CHELSEA HOUSE PUBLISHERS
NEW YORK
PHILADELPHIA

Chelsea House Publishers
EDITOR-IN-CHIEF: Nancy Toff
EXECUTIVE EDITOR: Remmel T. Nunn
MANAGING EDITOR: Karyn Gullen Browne
COPY CHIEF: Juliann Barbato
PICTURE EDITOR: Adrian G. Allen
ART DIRECTOR: Maria Epes
MANUFACTURING MANAGER: Gerald Levine

World Leaders—Past & Present
SENIOR EDITOR: John W. Selfridge

Staff for KHOMEINI
ASSOCIATE EDITOR: Jeff Klein
ASSISTANT EDITOR: Bert Yaeger
DEPUTY COPY CHIEF: Mark Rifkin
EDITORIAL ASSISTANT: Nate Eaton
PICTURE RESEARCHERS: Kathy Bonomi, Elizabeth Terhune, Brian Araujo
ASSISTANT ART DIRECTOR: Loraine Machlin
DESIGNER: Irene Friedman
ASSISTANT DESIGNER: James Baker
PRODUCTION MANAGER: Joseph Romano
PRODUCTION COORDINATOR: Marie Claire Cebrián
COVER ILLUSTRATION: Jim Harter

Second Revised Edition

3 5 7 9 8 6 4

Library of Congress Cataloging-in-Publication Data

Gordon, Matthew. KHOMEINI.

(World leaders past & present)
Bibliography: p.
Includes index.
1. Khomeini, Ruhollah—Juvenile literature. 2. Iran—
History—1979–   —Juvenile literature.
[1. Khomeini, Ruhollah. 2. Islam—Biography. 3. Iran—
History—1979–   ] I. Title. II. Series.
DS318.84.K48G67   1986   955'.054'0924 [B] [92] 86-14764

ISBN 0-87754-559-6
      0-7910-0583-6 (pbk.)

Contents

WORLD LEADERS   PAST & PRESENT

John Adams
John Quincy Adams
Konrad Adenauer
Alexander the Great
Salvador Allende
Marc Antony
Corazon Aquino
Yasir Arafat
King Arthur
Hafez al-Assad
Kemal Atatürk
Attila
Clement Attlee
Augustus Caesar
Menachem Begin
David Ben-Gurion
Otto von Bismarck
Léon Blum
Simon Bolívar
Cesare Borgia
Willy Brandt
Leonid Brezhnev
Julius Caesar
John Calvin
Jimmy Carter
Fidel Castro
Catherine the Great
Charlemagne
Chiang Kai-Shek
Winston Churchill
Georges Clemenceau
Cleopatra
Constantine the Great
Hernán Cortés
Oliver Cromwell
Georges-Jacques
  Danton
Jefferson Davis
Moshe Dayan
Charles de Gaulle
Eamon De Valera
Eugene Debs
Deng Xiaoping
Benjamin Disraeli
Alexander Dubček
François & Jean-Claude
  Duvalier
Dwight Eisenhower
Eleanor of Aquitaine
Elizabeth I
Faisal
Ferdinand & Isabella
Francisco Franco
Benjamin Franklin

Frederick the Great
Indira Gandhi
Mohandas Gandhi
Giuseppe Garibaldi
Amin & Bashir Gemayel
Genghis Khan
William Gladstone
Mikhail Gorbachev
Ulysses S. Grant
Ernesto "Che" Guevara
Tenzin Gyatso
Alexander Hamilton
Dag Hammarskjöld
Henry VIII
Henry of Navarre
Paul von Hindenburg
Hirohito
Adolf Hitler
Ho Chi Minh
King Hussein
Ivan the Terrible
Andrew Jackson
James I
Wojciech Jaruzelski
Thomas Jefferson
Joan of Arc
Pope John XXIII
Pope John Paul II
Lyndon Johnson
Benito Juárez
John Kennedy
Robert Kennedy
Jomo Kenyatta
Ayatollah Khomeini
Nikita Khrushchev
Kim Il Sung
Martin Luther King, Jr.
Henry Kissinger
Kublai Khan
Lafayette
Robert E. Lee
Vladimir Lenin
Abraham Lincoln
David Lloyd George
Louis XIV
Martin Luther
Judas Maccabeus
James Madison
Nelson & Winnie
  Mandela
Mao Zedong
Ferdinand Marcos
George Marshall

Mary, Queen of Scots
Tomáš Masaryk
Golda Meir
Klemens von Metternich
James Monroe
Hosni Mubarak
Robert Mugabe
Benito Mussolini
Napoléon Bonaparte
Gamal Abdel Nasser
Jawaharlal Nehru
Nero
Nicholas II
Richard Nixon
Kwame Nkrumah
Daniel Ortega
Mohammed Reza Pahlavi
Thomas Paine
Charles Stewart
  Parnell
Pericles
Juan Perón
Peter the Great
Pol Pot
Muammar el-Qaddafi
Ronald Reagan
Cardinal Richelieu
Maximilien Robespierre
Eleanor Roosevelt
Franklin Roosevelt
Theodore Roosevelt
Anwar Sadat
Haile Selassie
Prince Sihanouk
Jan Smuts
Joseph Stalin
Sukarno
Sun Yat-sen
Tamerlane
Mother Teresa
Margaret Thatcher
Josip Broz Tito
Toussaint L'Ouverture
Leon Trotsky
Pierre Trudeau
Harry Truman
Queen Victoria
Lech Walesa
George Washington
Chaim Weizmann
Woodrow Wilson
Xerxes
Emiliano Zapata
Zhou Enlai

CHELSEA HOUSE PUBLISHERS

ON LEADERSHIP

Arthur M. Schlesinger, jr.

LEADERSHIP, it may be said, is really what makes the world go round. Love no doubt smooths the passage; but love is a private transaction between consenting adults. Leadership is a public transaction with history. The idea of leadership affirms the capacity of individuals to move, inspire, and mobilize masses of people so that they act together in pursuit of an end. Sometimes leadership serves good purposes, sometimes bad; but whether the end is benign or evil, great leaders are those men and women who leave their personal stamp on history.

Now, the very concept of leadership implies the proposition that individuals can make a difference. This proposition has never been universally accepted. From classical times to the present day, eminent thinkers have regarded individuals as no more than the agents and pawns of larger forces, whether the gods and goddesses of the ancient world or, in the modern era, race, class, nation, the dialectic, the will of the people, the spirit of the times, history itself. Against such forces, the individual dwindles into insignificance.

So contends the thesis of historical determinism. Tolstoy's great novel *War and Peace* offers a famous statement of the case. Why, Tolstoy asked, did millions of men in the Napoleonic Wars, denying their human feelings and their common sense, move back and forth across Europe slaughtering their fellows? "The war," Tolstoy answered, "was bound to happen simply because it was bound to happen." All prior history predetermined it. As for leaders, they, Tolstoy said, "are but the labels that serve to give a name to an end and, like labels, they have the least possible connection with the event." The greater the leader, "the more conspicuous the inevitability and the predestination of every act he commits." The leader, said Tolstoy, is "the slave of history."

Determinism takes many forms. Marxism is the determinism of class. Nazism the determinism of race. But the idea of men and women as the slaves of history runs athwart the deepest human instincts. Rigid determinism abolishes the idea of human freedom—

the assumption of free choice that underlies every move we make, every word we speak, every thought we think. It abolishes the idea of human responsibility, since it is manifestly unfair to reward or punish people for actions that are by definition beyond their control. No one can live consistently by any deterministic creed. The Marxist states prove this themselves by their extreme susceptibility to the cult of leadership.

More than that, history refutes the idea that individuals make no difference. In December 1931 a British politician crossing Park Avenue in New York City between 76th and 77th Streets around 10:30 P.M. looked in the wrong direction and was knocked down by an automobile—a moment, he later recalled, of a man aghast, a world aglare: "I do not understand why I was not broken like an eggshell or squashed like a gooseberry." Fourteen months later an American politician, sitting in an open car in Miami, Florida, was fired on by an assassin; the man beside him was hit. Those who believe that individuals make no difference to history might well ponder whether the next two decades would have been the same had Mario Constasino's car killed Winston Churchill in 1931 and Giuseppe Zangara's bullet killed Franklin Roosevelt in 1933. Suppose, in addition, that Adolf Hitler had been killed in the street fighting during the Munich *Putsch* of 1923 and that Lenin had died of typhus during World War I. What would the 20th century be like now?

For better or for worse, individuals do make a difference. "The notion that a people can run itself and its affairs anonymously," wrote the philosopher William James, "is now well known to be the silliest of absurdities. Mankind does nothing save through initiatives on the part of inventors, great or small, and imitation by the rest of us—these are the sole factors in human progress. Individuals of genius show the way, and set the patterns, which common people then adopt and follow."

Leadership, James suggests, means leadership in thought as well as in action. In the long run, leaders in thought may well make the greater difference to the world. But, as Woodrow Wilson once said, "Those only are leaders of men, in the general eye, who lead in action. . . . It is at their hands that new thought gets its translation into the crude language of deeds." Leaders in thought often invent in solitude and obscurity, leaving to later generations the tasks of imitation. Leaders in action—the leaders portrayed in this series—have to be effective in their own time.

And they cannot be effective by themselves. They must act in response to the rhythms of their age. Their genius must be adapted, in a phrase of William James's, "to the receptivities of the moment." Leaders are useless without followers. "There goes the mob," said the French politician hearing a clamor in the streets. "I am their leader. I must follow them." Great leaders turn the inchoate emotions of the mob to purposes of their own. They seize on the opportunities of their time, the hopes, fears, frustrations, crises, potentialities. They succeed when events have prepared the way for them, when the community is awaiting to be aroused, when they can provide the clarifying and organizing ideas. Leadership ignites the circuit between the individual and the mass and thereby alters history.

It may alter history for better or for worse. Leaders have been responsible for the most extravagant follies and most monstrous crimes that have beset suffering humanity. They have also been vital in such gains as humanity has made in individual freedom, religious and racial tolerance, social justice, and respect for human rights.

There is no sure way to tell in advance who is going to lead for good and who for evil. But a glance at the gallery of men and women in *World Leaders—Past and Present* suggests some useful tests.

One test is this: Do leaders lead by force or by persuasion? By command or by consent? Through most of history leadership was exercised by the divine right of authority. The duty of followers was to defer and to obey. "Theirs not to reason why / Theirs but to do and die." On occasion, as with the so-called enlightened despots of the 18th century in Europe, absolutist leadership was animated by humane purposes. More often, absolutism nourished the passion for domination, land, gold, and conquest and resulted in tyranny.

The great revolution of modern times has been the revolution of equality. The idea that all people should be equal in their legal condition has undermined the old structure of authority, hierarchy, and deference. The revolution of equality has had two contrary effects on the nature of leadership. For equality, as Alexis de Tocqueville pointed out in his great study *Democracy in America*, might mean equality in servitude as well as equality in freedom.

"I know of only two methods of establishing equality in the political world," Tocqueville wrote. "Rights must be given to every citizen, or none at all to anyone . . . save one, who is the master of all." There was no middle ground "between the sovereignty of all and the absolute power of one man." In his astonishing prediction of 20th-century totalitarian dictatorship, Tocqueville explained how the revolution of equality could lead to the *"Führerprinzip"* and more terrible absolutism than the world had ever known.

But when rights are given to every citizen and the sovereignty of all is established, the problem of leadership takes a new form, becomes more exacting than ever before. It is easy to issue commands and enforce them by the rope and the stake, the concentration camp and the *gulag.* It is much harder to use argument and achievement to overcome opposition and win consent. The Founding Fathers of the United States understood the difficulty. They believed that history had given them the opportunity to decide, as Alexander Hamilton wrote in the first Federalist Paper, whether men are indeed capable of basing government on "reflection and choice, or whether they are forever destined to depend . . . on accident and force."

Government by reflection and choice called for a new style of leadership and a new quality of followership. It required leaders to be responsive to popular concerns, and it required followers to be active and informed participants in the process. Democracy does not eliminate emotion from politics; sometimes it fosters demagoguery; but it is confident that, as the greatest of democratic leaders put it, you cannot fool all of the people all of the time. It measures leadership by results and retires those who overreach or falter or fail.

It is true that in the long run despots are measured by results too. But they can postpone the day of judgment, sometimes indefinitely, and in the meantime they can do infinite harm. It is also true that democracy is no guarantee of virtue and intelligence in government, for the voice of the people is not necessarily the voice of God. But democracy, by assuring the right of opposition, offers built-in resistance to the evils inherent in absolutism. As the theologian Reinhold Niebuhr summed it up, "Man's capacity for justice makes democracy possible, but man's inclination to injustice makes democracy necessary."

A second test for leadership is the end for which power is sought. When leaders have as their goal the supremacy of a master race or the promotion of totalitarian revolution or the acquisition and exploitation of colonies or the protection of greed and privilege or the preservation of personal power, it is likely that their leadership will do little to advance the cause of humanity. When their goal is the abolition of slavery, the liberation of women, the enlargement of opportunity for the poor and powerless, the extension of equal rights to racial minorities, the defense of the freedoms of expression and opposition, it is likely that their leadership will increase the sum of human liberty and welfare.

Leaders have done great harm to the world. They have also conferred great benefits. You will find both sorts in this series. Even "good" leaders must be regarded with a certain wariness. Leaders are not demigods; they put on their trousers one leg after another just like ordinary mortals. No leader is infallible, and every leader needs to be reminded of this at regular intervals. Irreverence irritates leaders but is their salvation. Unquestioning submission corrupts leaders and demeans followers. Making a cult of a leader is always a mistake. Fortunately hero worship generates its own antidote. "Every hero," said Emerson, "becomes a bore at last."

The signal benefit the great leaders confer is to embolden the rest of us to live according to our own best selves, to be active, insistent, and resolute in affirming our own sense of things. For great leaders attest to the reality of human freedom against the supposed inevitabilities of history. And they attest to the wisdom and power that may lie within the most unlikely of us, which is why Abraham Lincoln remains the supreme example of great leadership. A great leader, said Emerson, exhibits new possibilities to all humanity. "We feed on genius. . . . Great men exist that there may be greater men."

Great leaders, in short, justify themselves by emancipating and empowering their followers. So humanity struggles to master its destiny, remembering with Alexis de Tocqueville: "It is true that around every man a fatal circle is traced beyond which he cannot pass; but within the wide verge of that circle he is powerful and free; as it is with man, so with communities."

1

The Fall of the Embassy

Sunday, November 4, 1979, was a rainy, overcast day in Tehran. For months the city had been at the center of a violent revolution. Many had died, destruction was widespread, and tensions were high. Moorhead C. Kennedy, Jr., an economic counselor and one of the high-ranking diplomatic officers at the American Embassy, stood looking down from the window of his office, across the yard of the embassy compound. Beyond the wrought-iron gates that stood at the entrance to the compound, an angry crowd was massed on Takht-e Jamshid Avenue. It was chanting slogans denouncing the United States and Mohammed Reza Pahlavi, the Shah of Iran, who had been in power since 1941. "Death to the Shah, death to Carter, death to America," the shouts rang out.

The Shah's regime had grown increasingly oppressive since the 1960s, and had been responsible for the development of severe economic problems. The combination of these led to the emergence of a strong opposition movement. Because of its firm support for the Shah, the United States had also become a target of opposition.

All Western governments are just thieves. Nothing but evil comes from them.
—AYATOLLAH KHOMEINI

Chanting "Death to the Shah, death to America," angry crowds carry placards ridiculing the Shah of Iran, Mohammed Reza Pahlavi, and the United States. Demonstrators surrounded the U.S. Embassy in Tehran, Iran, shortly after youthful followers of Ayatollah Khomeini, leader of the Islamic Republic of Iran, seized 53 American hostages there on November 4, 1979.

AP/WIDE WORLD

Moorhead Kennedy, when interviewed later by journalists, said, "I remember looking down on all the noise and anti-American anger, and I wondered to myself what it would be like to die."

The crowd, made up of young students, both men and women, had demonstrated in front of the embassy for days. Their anger and bitterness against the Shah and the American government were evident. American flags were burned and pictures of the Shah and Jimmy Carter were trampled on. Throughout the crowd, people were waving pictures of a bearded, intense-looking man. Widely known in Iran, Ayatollah Ruhollah Khomeini was virtually unheard of in many parts of the world.

His face quickly became familiar in the West after the Islamic Revolution. The posters of the period capture the Khomeini aura well. His was the face of an elderly man, with a full white beard touched slightly with black. The forehead was broad and lined with furrows, the ears full, the black turban a sign of distinction. The eyes, the feature most often noted by those who had met Khomeini, were clear and dark. Beneath the bushy eyebrows, these eyes had a penetrating quality, the first in-

Atop the U.S. Embassy in Iran, militiamen of the Islamic Republic of Iran tear apart an American flag. Most participants in the embassy takeover were university students from middle-class backgrounds. Loyal to Khomeini, the young Iranians were members of such groups as the *Khat-e Imam*, or Students Following the Line of the Imam.

AP/WIDE WORLD

dication of Khomeini's intelligence and stubborn determination.

At the time of the embassy takeover, Khomeini was 77 years old and had recently had several episodes of poor health. On February 1, 1979, he had returned to Iran after 15 years of exile. During several years in Iraq, then in France, he had become the symbol and the leader of the revolutionary opposition movement that would, in 1979, overthrow the increasingly unpopular government of the Shah. On his return to Iran he was welcomed by a crowd of more than 2 million people. He set out immediately to alter radically the political and social foundations of Iran. Nine months later, in November, this revolution swept into the U.S. Embassy.

Three hours after Kennedy turned from his office window, on that Sunday morning, a Marine guard, part of the 13-man Marine contingent assigned to protect the enormous embassy compound, burst into Kennedy's office shouting that the embassy was

Members of the United States Embassy staff in Tehran are hustled to the U.S. ambassador's residence by their Iranian captors, beginning the 444-day Iranian hostage crisis. Khomeini's Islamic revolutionary regime, which had been established earlier in 1979, hoped this measure would discourage U.S. military intervention in Iran.

being taken over. Just after 10:00 A.M., large numbers of protesters scaled the embassy walls, breached the gates, and streamed into the compound. Most were armed with clubs or pipes. A few carried pistols.

At the time, most of the Americans were in the chancery, the main building of the embassy. As the crowd of Iranians broke through the doors of the chancery, the Marine guards, under orders not to use their weapons, tried to hold off their attackers with tear gas, slowing the attackers' momentum for a few seconds. Upstairs, locked in a top-secret vault room containing intelligence documents and communications equipment, a small group of Americans was hurriedly shredding documents. Others were smashing the delicate machines.

Elsewhere in the embassy, a number of Americans had been seized, several of them beaten. They were tied and blindfolded and rushed out to the yard. The Iranians in the chancery, realizing what was going on inside the locked vault, tried to break in. When this failed, they threatened to kill several of their prisoners unless those inside surrendered.

Iranian demonstrators at the U.S. Embassy shout *"Marg bar Carter"* ("Death to Carter"). During the protests in the final weeks of 1979, quotations from Khomeini were put up on the embassy's walls and Iranian demonstrators burned American flags. The angry protestors defaced portraits of U.S. President Jimmy Carter and the exiled Shah of Iran, then seeking medical treatment in the United States.

AP/WIDE WORLD

UPI/BETTMANN NEWSPHOTOS

During a heated confrontation in Washington, D.C., between American and pro-Khomeini Iranian demonstrators, an American hangs a mask of Khomeini in effigy. Virtually unknown to the general public in the United States until the Iranian hostage crisis, Khomeini's image filled many Americans with outrage and contempt.

The Americans gave in, and, on emerging from the vault, were tied like the others and taken to the embassy yard. All the prisoners were gathered together and marched to the ambassador's residence, where they were tied to chairs.

Thus began for 53 Americans a 444-day ordeal known as the Iranian hostage crisis. For the hostages and their families it was a period full of fear, loneliness, and uncertainty.

President Jimmy Carter informs the press in May 1980 of the Iranian government's decision to take custody of the U.S. hostages, calling it a "positive step" toward ending the long ordeal for the hostages and their families. In 1977 Carter had told the Shah that Iran was an "oasis of stability."

UPI/BETTMANN NEWSPHOTOS

The majority of the group that took the embassy were students from middle-class families. Most were students of engineering, medicine, chemistry, and mathematics. Roughly one-quarter were women. With a few exceptions they came from two of the largest universities in Tehran, the Polytechnic School and the University of Tehran.

Many of these students had first met at the university in political and religious meetings. They had been active in the movement against the Shah, which had emerged in the 1960s and early 1970s. In 1979 they were the core of a new Islamic organization, called the *Khat-e Imam*, or Students Following the Line of the Imam, which was formed at the University of Tehran and the Polytechnic School. The title *Imam* referred to Ayatollah Khomeini. The term *ayatollah* means "miraculous sign of God," and is used in an unofficial way to refer to an individual perceived to be a top-ranking religious figure. The title is usually earned on the basis of both scholarship and religious standing.

Khomeini had become the focus of these students' loyalty. His teachings were studied and discussed, as were the significant events of his life. Sayings from Khomeini's writings and speeches were emblazoned on banners and hung on the walls of the captured American Embassy. Only hours after the takeover, one of the students gave an interview to Tehran Radio in which he made an offhand remark that the operation had been planned some days in advance. A similar statement was also made by an official close to Khomeini in the new revolutionary government.

The man who served as both a leader for the students and a link between them and Khomeini's inner circle was Mohammed Musavi Khoeiniha. He had worked as Khomeini's representative among student groups in Tehran.

Mohammed Khoeiniha was close to the inner cir-

UPI/BETTMANN NEWSPHOTOS

Mohammed Musavi Khoeiniha speaking to crowds from the U.S. Embassy wall following the takeover by militant Iranian students. Khoeiniha, one of Khomeini's closest advisers, read a statement from the ayatollah (Khomeini's title, meaning "miraculous sign of God"), expressing his support for the students' actions.

cle of Khomeini's advisers, and was also a friend of Ahmed Khomeini, one of the ayatollah's sons. On November 5, the day after the takeover, Ahmed Khomeini not only visited the embassy, he also read to the students a message from Khomeini. In the message the ayatollah praised the action and encouraged the students to stand firm. It is not clear whether Khomeini helped plan the embassy takeover, but he did support it from the first day, and would continue to support it, even when some of his aides began to criticize the action.

For the United States, the hostage crisis was a foreign policy catastrophe. For President Jimmy Carter, the release of the 53 hostages became the immediate and pressing goal of his administration. To achieve this end, negotiations and, later, economic and political pressures were tried. All of these failed. Frustrated, Carter turned to the military and, in April 1980, a rescue operation was launched which resulted in failure and the deaths of eight

Burnt-out aircraft and the charred remains of U.S. military personnel marked the grim conclusion of a mission ordered on April 25, 1980, by President Carter to rescue the American hostages held in Tehran. American aircraft and helicopters crashed over the Iranian desert, 200 miles from their destination.

UPI/BETTMANN NEWSPHOTOS

American servicemen. The crisis then entered a complex period of negotiations involving several governments. These talks dragged on for nine months until, in January 1981, coinciding with Ronald Reagan's inauguration as president of the United States, the hostages were freed. Many Americans had found the crisis a deeply frustrating and humiliating experience for the United States. As for Carter, this crisis, as he and his advisers would later admit, was one of the main reasons for his failure to win a second term as president.

For the Iranians, however, in the midst of a divisive revolution, the hostage crisis meant something different. The takeover had been presented, first, as an attempt to force the return of the Shah, who had been admitted to the United States for medical treatment in October 1979, and, second, as a way of protesting the involvement of the United States in Iranian affairs.

Ex-hostages Jerry Plotkin (top), Robert Ode (second from top), and another American arrive in West Germany on January 21, 1981, after the Iranian government released all American captives. For President Carter, the hostage crisis damaged his chances for reelection, while for Khomeini's government, it forcefully protested years of U.S. involvement in Iranian affairs.

21

2

The Child and the Prophet

Ruhollah Khomeini was born, probably in 1902, in Khomein, a tiny village in Iran, which was then called Persia. It was from this village that Khomeini would later take his name. Situated on the edge of the bleak Iranian desert, Khomein is a dusty, remote oasis. The name Khomein is an odd mixture of Persian and Arabic, and means "two jars." It is not known for certain where it came from. One story has it that in the 7th century an Arab military commander, part of the Muslim army spreading Islam into Iran, arrived at this small oasis with his troops. He ordered that two huge jars be filled with local beverages. These were then given to his troops, now parched from their trek in the desert. The Arab troops later departed but the name remained, according to the story.

Khomeini was born into a poor family that claimed special status as being descended from the prophet Muhammad, the founder of the Islamic religion. Such a status carries with it certain privileges. When addressing such persons, it is customary to use the title *sayid* for men, and *sayidah* for women. And the men who belong to this

---

Muslim women wearing traditional dark robes, called *chadors* in Persian, walk through a corridor leading to the tomb of the prophet Muhammad in Medina, Saudi Arabia, where the founder of the Islamic faith died in 632 A.D. Khomeini's grandfather held the title *sayid*, signifying that he was a descendant of Muhammad.

A typical Western image of the prophet Muhammad. Born in 570 A.D., Muhammad began preaching in the Arab commercial town of Mecca after receiving divine revelations. Muhammad's disciples became the first followers of Islam. Like Judaism and Christianity, Islam maintains belief in one God.

group — Khomeini included — always wear a black turban. There were, and continue to be, many such families in Iranian society.

Sayid Ahmed, Khomeini's grandfather, arrived with his family in Khomein around 1840. He was born in Kashmir, India, but was sent by his father to the northern Iranian city of Nishapur for his education. There he married and settled until moving to Khomein. Having received full religious education in Nishapur, he was a learned man. He was therefore known in the community as a *mullah*.

Common in Iran, the term mullah refers to someone who is perceived by those around him to be well-trained in religious matters. It is used loosely, however, and does not always refer to a formally educated man. A mullah in a poor village might barely have learned to read and write, but can recite verses from the Koran. The Koran is the holy text of Islam. The name might also be used for a scholar of considerable learning in an urban center who participates fully in the intellectual life around him.

Little is known about Sayid Ahmed's life. He seems to have been financially fairly well-off. As can be expected of a man with his background, he was concerned about the education of his children, especially his sons, including Mostafa, Khomeini's father. They received a religious education from Sayid Ahmed, and Mostafa, too, became a mullah. When Sayid Ahmed died, his property was divided among his family members. Following this, the family seems to have lost its wealth. They were forced to live as sharecroppers, depending on the land to feed and support them. But Khomein lay near the desert; the soil was poor, and so the family must often have gone hungry.

In 1887 Mostafa, now a young man, married Sadiqeh, the daughter of a local landlord. She was perhaps not even 12 years old when she married, which was not an unusual age for girls at that time to be wed. They had several children over the next few years, only one of which, Murtaza, survived childhood. Then, probably in November of 1902, the family's second son, Ruhollah, was born. He would become the man known as Ayatollah Khomeini.

Soon after Khomeini's birth his father was murdered, for reasons that remain unclear. According to one story, he became involved in an argument with two men sent by the landlord to collect the rent. Sayid Mostafa, feeling perhaps the sum was more than he could afford to pay, refused. The men argued and Mostafa was stabbed to death. It may also have been that Khomeini's father was really killed by bandits, who are known to have frequented that area of Iran.

Fatherless before his first birthday, the child was sent to live with his aunt by his mother, now too poor to support the whole family.

THE METROPOLITAN MUSEUM OF ART, ROGERS FUND, 1940

A leaf from a 13th-century Persian (or Iranian) copy of the Koran, the holy text of Islam, emblazoned with ornate gold calligraphy. The Koran's teachings are thought to encompass all aspects of life. The son of a *mullah* (a man considered knowledgeable in religious matters), Khomeini began studying the Koran as a small child.

A 19th-century Iranian illustration depicts Muhammad ascending into heaven. Forced to move his community from Mecca to Medina, Muhammad is sometimes compared with Moses, the Biblical leader and prophet. Khomeini wears the black turban of the *sayids,* those believed to be descended from the prophet Muhammad.

The four-year-old was sent from Khomein in 1906 to start his formal education. Despite the hardships he and his family endured, Khomeini had received the early education expected of a mullah's son. According to his brother, who was interviewed later by an Iranian journalist, Khomeini was always an attentive and intelligent student.

Like many Iranian children of the time, Khomeini began his education by learning the Koran. This text is used in Muslim societies to teach children to read, recite, and, by copying out verses of the book, to write. As in many parts of the Muslim world, small schools exist just for this purpose. What is vital about the Koran is not only that it is the word of God, but that it contains teachings about many important aspects of life — personal, social, political, and religious. The Koran was thought of in this way during the days of Islam's earliest followers.

Islam was the last of the three great monotheistic religions — those that accept only one god — the earlier two being Judaism and Christianity. Today, it is practiced by roughly 700 to 800 million people in more than 60 countries, including nations in the Far East and Middle East, and in large communities in the Soviet Union, Europe, and the United States.

In the first decades of the 7th century, Mecca was a commercial center for the merchant caravans that crossed the Arabian peninsula. It was in Mecca that Muhammad ibn Abd Allah, a member of the Arabian tribe of Quraysh, began to spread the messages of the new faith.

Muhammad, who is revered by all Muslims as the prophet of Islam, was born around 570 A.D. Orphaned at a young age, Muhammad spent his early adulthood as a merchant. At the age of 40, it is believed, he received his first revelation from God, whom Muslims call *Allah* in Arabic. Muhammad began to preach in Mecca and attracted a small group of disciples. He continued to preach and to receive revelations. The small group of Muslims increased in numbers. However, Muhammad was viewed by other Meccans as a threat to the existing religious and social order. Opposition to him grew increasingly violent.

In 622, because of this violence, Muhammad fled Mecca and made his way to the nearby town of Medina. There he was met by the other Muslims, ones whom he had sent ahead earlier. Medina thus became the first center of this new religion. It was in Medina that Muhammad emerged not only as a religious, but as a political and military leader as well. In this way he was similar to the Biblical prophet Moses, who was also both the religious head of his community and its military and political chief.

In 630 Muhammad returned to Mecca at the head of a number of followers. From that point on, Mecca assumed a central importance in Islam. For it is there that all Muslims, if possible, should travel in order to perform a set of sacred rituals. This pilgrimage, which is now administered by the Saudi Arabian government, is called the *hajj*.

In 632 Muhammad suddenly died. He left behind him a fledgling community of Muslims now deprived of his leadership.

Muslims in the desert recite daily prayers as they face toward Mecca, where Muhammad began gathering followers in the 7th century. For Khomeini, Islamic law applies to man "before the embryo is formed until after he is placed in the tomb."

To answer political and legal questions, as well as religious ones, early Muslims could turn to the set of revelations brought forth by God through Muhammad. According to Muslim tradition, these had been recorded during Muhammad's lifetime and organized into chapters. After Muhammad's death, a further organization of these chapters was carried out. From this emerged the Koran.

To shed light on the meaning of this difficult book, Muslims look to the collection of personal sayings of Muhammad and reports of his activities, called *hadith*. They constitute the *Sunnah* of the prophet Muhammad. Sunnah means "sacred custom," and for Muslims, this collection of reports represents another source of religious truth. The Koran and the Sunnah do not address only religious matters. They also address such concerns as marriage, inheritance, and taxes.

Ayatollah Khomeini, like many Muslims, believed that Islam is the source of basic rules regulating the important aspects of people's lives.

In a lesson Khomeini would later give as a teacher he would say this about Islam: "God instituted laws and practices for all human affairs and laid down injunctions for man extending from even before the embryo is formed until after he is placed in the tomb." This conviction lies at the heart of Khomeini's ideas.

Little else is known of Khomeini's early years. However, when he was 16, two significant events occurred. A few months after the death of his aunt, his mother also died, and Ruhollah became an orphan. At the time, it seems he was living with his elder brother Murtaza. As was customary, the two of them observed a 40-day period of mourning for the two women.

In the sermons Khomeini would give as an adult, there are signs that he had thought deeply about his years of hardship and poverty. As he grew older, one of the lessons he would repeat was on the need to help society's poor and downtrodden. He later made the suffering of the poor a main point of criticism against the Shah.

At the Great Mosque in Mecca, Muslims surround the Kaaba, the first sanctuary for Muhammad and his disciples. Muslims from more than 60 countries make the pilgrimage called the *hajj*, commemorating Muhammad's return here in 630. In 1982 Khomeini told Iranians to "use the hajj for an Islamic uprising."

3

The Seeker

Khomeini left his brother's home in Khomein to continue his education when he was 16. According to one writer, this came after his teacher told him there was nothing left for him to learn in Khomein. It was time, he said, for Ruhollah to pursue his education elsewhere. He would have to become a *talebeh*. An Arabic word incorporated into Persian, the language of Iran, it originally meant "seeker." Today it refers to students who attend the *madreseh*, or religious school.

In the Islamic educational system several important fields are connected with the study of religion. One of the most important is jurisprudence, or laws and the study of their application. Throughout the history of Islam there has been a need for scholars who can read and explain these legal texts. These scholars are called *ulama*, an Arabic word meaning "men of religious learning." Because of their knowledge of law and religion, members of this highly respected group have traditionally provided the judges and legal experts for Muslim society.

With his brother's help, Khomeini considered his options. There were several centers of learning in Iran where he could go, including those in the cities of Mashhad and Tehran. After a short while he decided on the madreseh in the small city of Arak. Located roughly 140 miles southwest of Tehran, Arak was known for its orchards and mineral

I have told you all the things that I know, except one . . . and that one thing you must go and seek elsewhere. You must become a talebeh [student].
—SAYYED ABOL-HASSAN
Islamic teacher, to Khomeini before he left Khomein

A member of the *ulama*, or "men of religious learning," in Iran in the early 1900s. Around 1918 the 16-year-old *talebeh* (meaning "student") Ruhollah Khomeini attended the *madreseh*, or religious school, at Arak, Iran. In 1921 Abd al-Karim Ha'eri, the school's leader, brought his pupils to Qom.

UPI/BETTMANN NEWSPHOTOS

springs. The madreseh at Arak was headed by one of the leading teachers of the time, a scholar named Abd al-Karim Ha'eri. Ha'eri made a significant impression on the youthful Khomeini, though eventually Khomeini would break with this teacher's ideas.

Because of his learning and reputation, Ha'eri decided to leave the Arak school and move to the larger town of Qom. Khomeini accompanied him. Ha'eri's decision to move probably occurred because he felt Arak lacked the symbolic importance that would elevate his school's reputation. It was neither a major urban center nor a holy city.

At first glance there was little that was favorable about Qom. Located 100 miles south of Tehran, it was known for its desert climate, its often brackish water, and its generally dusty and inhospitable character. What drew Ha'eri, however, had nothing to do with climate.

A medium-sized town, Qom, at that time, lacked a theological school with a national reputation. There was a school there, one called the Faiziyeh, but it was not considered among the best in Iran. The school had looked for a scholar whose reputation would help the school become a first-rate institution. They wrote to Ha'eri, who was immediately interested in their offer. He knew that in Qom, in contrast to cities like Tehran and Mashhad, there were no other schools that might rival the Faiziyeh. It was also to his advantage that he could start teaching immediately. In 1921 he and some pupils moved to Qom and established themselves in the Faiziyeh. For Khomeini, the journey to Qom would eventually bring him to the leadership of the Islamic Revolution.

Considered one of the most holy cities in Iran, Qom was a place to which many thousands of pilgrims traveled yearly seeking the tomb of Fatimah Ma'sumah (Fatimah the Chaste), the sister of one of the most revered persons in Iranian Muslim history — Imam Ali al-Rida. (Khomeini's birthday is said to fall on the same day as Fatimah's.) Ali's tomb in Mashhad is also an important pilgrimage site for the Iranian Muslims.

The holy city of Qom in central Iran is the site of Muslim pilgrimages to the tomb of Fatimah Ma'sumah (Fatimah the Chaste), the sister of Ali al-Rida, a venerated figure in Islamic history. As Khomeini's headquarters inside Iran, Qom became the hub of the Islamic Revolution.

The death of the prophet Muhammad had left the early Muslims with the problem of who would be their next leader. At first, the senior members of the community decided to settle the matter by selecting one of their own group to lead. One group, however, disagreed, for in their opinion, Muhammad had named a successor.

This group believed that a man named Ali ibn Abu Talib had been appointed by Muhammad to succeed him as leader. Ali's father, Abu Talib, was the prophet's uncle and so Ali and Muhammad were cousins. Through his marriage to Muhammad's daughter Fatimah, Ali was also the prophet's son-in-law. While in Mecca, he became a close friend and adviser to the prophet. He also served as Muhammad's standard bearer in several important battles fought by the Muslims. He was, therefore, a leading member of the early community.

The episode most often associated with Ali and Muhammad took place at Ghadir Khumm, a small oasis between Mecca and Medina. At one time during his last years, Muhammad, accompanied by Ali and a group of leading Muslims, was returning to Medina after the pilgrimage to Mecca. At Ghadir Khumm, Muhammad stopped the caravan. There, he made a small pile of camel saddles. He stepped up onto this makeshift platform, looked at his companions, motioned to Ali, and took him by the hand. He then said, "Am I not master over all of the believers?" They replied, "Yes!" "Then," he continued, "for all those over whom I am master, Ali is also master. Oh God! Support all who support Ali and oppose all who oppose him."

For Ali and his followers, the meaning of this was clear: Ali, after Muhammad's death, was to become the new head of the community. The Shi'ite Muslim community (Shi'a) forms the second largest Muslim sect to survive Islam's long and complex history. This group comprises the vast majority of Muslims in Iran, and Shi'ites are also present in large numbers in Iraq, Lebanon, India, and Kuwait. The Shi'ites hold the story of Ghadir Khumm to be true, and, as a result, they have made Ali's claim as the rightful heir to the prophet Muhammad a crucial part of their dogma.

The other leading Muslims supported a man named Abu Bakr after Muhammad's death. The position of leader changed hands three times. Ali was overlooked after Abu Bakr's death. For his followers, who were still few in number, this was a mistake. In protest they adopted positions against the majority, from which emerged Shi'ite political and religious doctrines.

The great majority of Muslims belong to what is called Sunni Islam or Sunnism, often called "orthodox" Islam. Many other branches, or sects, emerged from Islam.

Although the Koran requires that Muslims pray three times daily to Allah (tradition asks for five times), and other exacting devotional rituals, certain sects stress severe physical self-denial and punishment. In this late 19th-century photograph a group of Muslims beat themselves, while one man displays heavy ornaments that hang from sharp hooks embedded in his skin.

UPI/BETTMANN NEWSPHOTOS

Iranian Shi'ite Muslims strike themselves during a remembrance of Husayn's murder by other Muslims in 680. One of the *imams*, or the heirs to Muhammad's authority, Husayn became an important Shi'ite martyr. Khomeini was raised a "Twelver" Shi'ite, named for the Twelfth, or Hidden, Imam, who disappeared in the 9th century and is expected to return before Judgment Day.

In 656, 24 years after the death of Muhammad, Ali was finally chosen to lead the Muslim faith. By this time Ali was facing opposition from other groups in the community. In 661, in the midst of war with various factions, Ali was stabbed and, two days later, died of his wounds.

With Ali's death, the Shi'a felt his status as the rightful successor to the prophet passed down to his eldest son Hasan. Hasan died in 669, and many of the Shi'a then turned to his younger brother Husayn. By this time, Islam had spread beyond the Arabian peninsula. Arab armies had conquered a vast area that included Egypt, Syria, Iraq, and Persia.

At the time of Hasan's death the ruler of the Islamic Empire was Yazid ibn Mu'awiyah. For the

Shi'a, Yazid became the symbol of cruel and despotic rulership. Centuries later, Khomeini would compare the Shah of Iran to Yazid, and the Shah's military forces to Yazid's army. Such a comparison was understood and quickly accepted by many Iranians during the Islamic Revolution.

By the 670s the Iraqi city of Kufah was a center of Shi'ite activity. The Shi'a there promised to support Husayn if he would rise up against Yazid and claim his rightful place as leader. Husayn, braving the dangers that awaited him, decided to travel to Kufah to raise support. He left his home in Mecca, with his infant son Ali Asghar, the rest of his family, and a handful of armed men.

On the way to Kufah, in October 680, at a place called Karbala, Husayn and his group encountered

A stone relief from the ancient Achaemenid dynasty in Persepolis, Iran, the city now called Takht-e Jamshid, founded by Darius I, the king, or Shah, of Persia from 521 to 486 B.C. Shah Mohammed Reza Pahlavi held a $120 million banquet here celebrating "2,500 years of Iranian kingship" in 1971. Khomeini denounced it as insensitive to Iran's poor.

an armed contingent sent by Yazid. These troops were ordered to prevent Husayn from reaching Kufah. Soon the contingent was joined by a small army. Yazid's troops surrounded Husayn and his people, and cut them off from the only available source of water, a nearby river. Though Husayn and the others fought bravely, they were outnumbered. Holding his baby son, who had been killed with an arrow in the throat, Husayn was the last to fall. His head was severed and sent to Damascus, along with women and children who were taken as prisoners. Seeing Husayn's bloody head, Yazid is said to have gloated.

For a number of years after Ali's death the Shi'a opposed those in power because they saw these rulers as corrupt and illegitimate. Yazid's murder of Husayn only showed them their view was correct. Against men like Yazid, they felt the only choice was resistance.

The largest of the Shi'a sects that formed, which is called the Twelver Shi'a, is the group to which Khomeini belongs. The Twelvers believe that after the deaths of Ali, Hasan, and Husayn, the rightful claim to leadership passed to Ali ibn Husayn, the only one of Husayn's sons to survive the massacre at Karbala.

The Twelvers believe this inheritance, passed down through the generations, was not only political in nature, but religious and intellectual as well. In their view, God Himself had chosen Muhammad and these select others to be the rightful leaders, so their qualities had a divine stamp, and these people were therefore faultless; Ali and this designated group of his descendants were incapable of sin or any error in political or legal judgment. The term given by the Shi'a to these individuals is *imam* — not to be confused with the same term when it is used for Khomeini. When the term Imam is applied to Khomeini it is in the more general sense of a political and religious leader, as it is used by all Muslims. In this instance, it is not used to mean one of the divinely chosen descendants of Ali and his two sons.

The Twelver Shi'a believe that after Ali, the First

Islam says that . . . the most exemplary and supreme form of struggle is that a man should stand before an oppressive leader and speak the word of justice.
—MORTEZA MOTAHARI

An intricate 16th-century Iranian silk rug from the Safavid period. The reign of the Safavid dynasty and the division of Islam in Iran into Sunni (orthodox) and Shi'ite Muslims began when Isma'il won control of the nation in 1501. Under Shah Isma'il, Twelver Shi'ism became the state religion.

Imam, there are 11 Imams. The Eighth Imam, whose sister is buried in Qom, is Ali al-Rida. The Eleventh Imam is Hasan al-'Askari. He, according to this branch of the Shi'ites, had a son, born in 869, named Muhammad al-Mahdi. This Muhammad is considered the Twelfth Imam, from which the group derived its name, "Twelver," or *Ithna Ashariya* in Arabic.

Many legends and stories of miracles grew up around the Twelfth Imam. He is thought to have gone into a small cave under a mosque in Samarra, Iraq, never to be seen again. For this reason, he is called the Hidden Imam by the Twelver Shi'a. It is believed that this Imam remains in hiding.

The Twelver Shi'a came to believe that in the future, before Judgment Day, the Hidden Imam will reappear. As the *Mahdi* (The One Led By God), he will head a powerful army, and completely destroy all the forces of evil in the world, including corrupt and oppressive governments. A thousand years of justice and peace will follow until the coming of Judgment Day.

The Shi'a rejected the legitimacy of any ruler who was not an Imam. Through the centuries, protest against any such ruler was seen to be acceptable. Most often, when the ruler was just in his policies, the Shi'a and their ulama would accept his rule without question. If a ruler showed himself to be cruel or corrupt, then the Twelvers turned to their doctrines and criticized the ruler for being unjust.

After the 16th century there were increasing examples of Shi'ite ulama who dared to speak out against oppressive rulers. They brought about a tradition of political activism. A later product of this tradition would be Khomeini himself. In building up opposition to the Shah, he would show himself to be a skilled political strategist.

A Muslim scholar at the Prophet's Mosque in Mecca, Saudi Arabia. Here, after Muhammad's death, his friend Abu Bakr declared that "God is living and undying." During the Safavid dynasty, the Shi'ite leadership established the scholarly rank of *mujtahid*, meaning "he who can offer guidance." In the 1960s Khomeini became a *marja'-i taqlid*, meaning "model for imitation."

41

4

The King and the Village

In 1501 Iran became a Shi'ite state when a man named Isma'il, having seized control of most of Iran, declared Twelver Shi'ism to be the state religion. After defeating the dynasty then ruling Iran, he declared himself to be Shah, and became the first ruler of the Safavid Shi'ite dynasty, which reigned over Iran until 1722. By the end of this two-century-long period the Safavids had ensured the nearly complete acceptance of Shi'ite Islam in northwest Iran.

At the start of Safavid rule, most Iranians were still Sunnis. Shah Isma'il and the rulers who came after him immediately set out to convert this population. This was accomplished, at least in the beginning, through force. The Safavids persecuted Sunni ulama, thus depriving the population of their religious leadership. The dynasty lacked a Shi'ite ulama large enough to support the state and help in expanding Shi'ite Islam.

To resolve this problem, Isma'il, and particularly his immediate successors, turned to the Shi'ite communities in Iraq, Syria, and Bahrain. There they found numbers of ulama who were willing to

If kings enter a village, they will despoil it, loot it, and turn its honorable inhabitants into slaves.
—from the Koran

Khomeini was a promising religious student at Qom in 1925 when the Qajar dynasty, which had ruled Iran since the 19th century, was toppled. The leader of the uprising, a successful soldier, crowned himself Reza Shah Pahlavi in 1926. Reza Shah changed his country's name from Persia to Iran in 1934, and began modernizing the country despite objections from the Islamic community.

move to Iran and work for the Safavid state. They came to Iran in increasing numbers throughout the 16th century. These ulama worked for the Safavid rulers as religious and legal advisers. The result of this policy was that the ulama were closely aligned with the state through the 16th and early 17th centuries. Beginning in the 18th century, however, the ulama of Iran gradually became an independent body in both the religious and political arenas. The alliance between the state and the ulama began to break down.

Since the Twelfth Imam had disappeared, a source of religious and political leadership had to be found. To meet this need there emerged among the ulama a type of scholar known as *mujtahid*. The term refers to scholars who are learned enough to make legal decisions. It was to these men that the Shi'a looked for religious and political direction.

The exceptional mujtahid may also reach a higher level — the *marja'-i taqlid*, or a "model for imitation." These are mujtahids who are recognized by other mullahs to be so qualified in law and religion that their example should be imitated. This is a difficult position to reach. It is rare, therefore, for there to be any more than a few of these "models."

With the rise of the Safavids, the Shi'ite ulama, especially the mujtahids, were in a new position. They were called on to participate in the running of a state. As men of religion, the ulama administered a religious institution called a *vakf*, which was a kind of endowment. From the vakf they gained a fixed and regular income, which enabled them to support themselves and their students. To this money many ulama could then add part of the funds they collected from the religious taxes. These were of two kinds. One was the *khums*, which is a tax of one-fifth of all net income. One-half of this tax goes to the state and one-half to the leading religious figure of the region. The other tax is called *zakat*, which is the alms money expected of all Muslims who can afford it. This money is distributed to the poor. However, it is first collected by the ulama, who are then responsible for its distribution. The end

Nasir ad-Din Shah, third of four Qajar dynasty rulers, governed Iran from 1848 to 1896. In 1890 he granted a British monopoly over Iranian tobacco, causing the Tobacco Rebellion after a Shi'ite scholar ruled against tobacco use. In 1905, angered by increased foreign interference, Shi'ite mullahs rebelled, and demanded a constitutional government.

result was that by the 20th century, the Iranian ulama had established for themselves an independent basis of power. Khomeini's eventual rise had much to do with the Shah and his father, Reza Shah, being unable to counter this independence.

Thus, over time, leading members of the ulama emerged as a wealthy and influential elite. For those ulama who chose to get involved in politics, they were now in a position to do so. Most ulama, however, including most leading mujtahids, completely avoided politics. In the 18th century, when Iran was taken over by the Qajar dynasty, a tradition of political activism among the ulama was born.

By the 19th century, Great Britain and Russia were becoming increasingly involved in Iranian affairs. They exercised a great deal of influence in Iranian politics and forced the Qajar rulers to adopt policies favorable to the Europeans. Their influence in the economy was especially significant. A series of commercial treaties benefited Iran (then still called Persia). However, the foreign merchants and representatives in the country were favored with "extraterritoriality," meaning that the Europeans within Iran were above Iranian law, a situation the ulama bitterly resented.

In 1890 the Qajar ruler, Nasir ad-Din Shah, granted a monopoly over the production and sale of Iranian tobacco to the British Imperial Tobacco Company. As word of this decision spread through Iran, the response was outrage. Iranians were convinced the Qajar rulers were trying to sell Iran off to foreign companies. By 1891 protests had broken out in Shiraz and Tabriz, then quickly spread to other cities. Many of the protests were led by local mullahs.

Hajj Murza Shiraze, the only marja'-i taqlid at that time, issued a legal ruling against the use of tobacco by Iranians. In an amazing display of unity, the majority of Iranians simply stopped smoking. The Tobacco Rebellion forced the government to cancel the British tobacco monopoly in early 1892. This protest represented the first successful mass movement in the modern history of Iran, with the ulama

A 15th-century Iranian miniature shows an old woman petitioning a ruler. Relations between the state and the Shi'ite ulama were often troubled. By the 17th century the ulama became more independent; during the 18th century, Shi'ite political activism increased — chiefly against foreign domination.

Workers in an Iranian tobacco field in the 1890s. Shi'ite mullahs forced the cancellation of the British tobacco monopoly in Iran in 1892 after the Shi'ite leader, Hajj Murza Shiraze, ruled that Iranians should stop smoking tobacco.

playing a major role in organizing it.

In the early 1900s new protests focused on the corruption of the Qajar state and Russian interference in Iranian affairs. Two huge loans from the Russian government had been accepted, and Russian merchants had been given a series of trade concessions.

Iranians had twice fought the tsar, the Russian monarch, in the early 1800s. In the late 19th century, the mullahs became increasingly hostile toward Russia, whose tsarist government was then annexing parts of northern Iran. In 1917 a communist Soviet government assumed power in Russia. The Russian communists, or Bolsheviks, rejected belief in God. The Soviets marched on Tehran in 1917 and forced further concessions from the Iranian government. The Shi'ites regarded the Soviets as a scourge against Islam.

More than a decade earlier, revolutionary groups began to form in Iran. In December 1905 a group of mullahs and leading merchants came forward against the government, initiating the Constitutional Revolution. They demanded a change in state policies, particularly regarding the Russians. Soon they demanded a representative assembly. Faced with such opposition, the Qajar ruler was forced to accept these measures. In 1906 and 1907 two important documents were put together by the new assembly. These documents formed the core of the first Iranian constitution — one that would last, mostly on paper, until the revolution of 1979.

For a young man such as Ruhollah Khomeini, the reforms of the early 1900s must have been attractive. A number of years would elapse, however, before Khomeini decided to take part actively in politics.

By 1923 Khomeini's teacher, Ha'eri, and his students were established in their new center in Qom. A few students, including Khomeini, became interested in a branch of study called *irfan,* the study of the mystical inner, or esoteric, side of the Koran and Islam. A very difficult field, having limited use to the general society, it was always considered a peripheral subject.

Khomeini, according to those who remember him at the madreseh, acquired a reputation as a serious, hardworking student. Because of this approach to his work, Khomeini remained one of Ha'eri's top pupils. The style of instruction in these schools was one of question and answer, argument and debate. Khomeini showed himself to be skilled at this kind of discussion. He knew how to ask probing questions and, when challenged, he could respond quickly and effectively. In the early 1930s he earned his diploma and went immediately into teaching.

Before long, Khomeini became a popular teacher.

Government soldiers during the Tobacco Rebellion of 1892. During the next quarter century further rebellions broke out against government corruption and the Russian occupation of Iranian territories. Demands in 1905 by Iran's mullahs and merchants forced the Qajar ruler to pass the country's first constitution. The constitution stood until Khomeini's 1979 revolution.

As was true for other instructors in the Faiziyeh school, Khomeini lectured on religious topics, jurisprudence, and philosophy. He also held a class for selected students in irfan, which was considered rather unusual — one reason why Khomeini gained a reputation for being unconventional. His class in ethics won him the greatest attention from the students.

This class attracted large numbers of students and soon became one of the most popular in the Faiziyeh. Khomeini encouraged his listeners to concentrate on developing their self-control and moral character. He also included in these lectures comments on social and political concerns.

Khomeini saw in Islam not only religious but also social responsibilities. As a former student of his later remarked, "Khomeini said the ulama had a responsibility for humanity not only in Iran but wherever people were hungry and oppressed." These were powerful words for the students.

Khomeini remained an instructor at the Faiziyeh in Qom until the early 1960s. For him, and for Iran, it was a time marked by crucial developments.

In 1937 Abd al-Karim Ha'eri died. Ha'eri had been successful not only in becoming one of Iran's leading scholars, but also in building the reputation of Qom and the Faiziyeh, as he had hoped. He used his wealth to build up the school, to found a hospital, and to put up new housing. Qom was becoming one of the top centers of Shi'ite learning in the world.

For seven years the Faiziyeh continued to operate, and, of course, the work for teachers like Khomeini never ceased. The need was felt for a new and respected scholar who could fill Ha'eri's shoes. In December 1944 a successor was found. His name was Ayatollah Mohammad Husayn Borujerdi, one of the leading mujtahids of Iran at the time. Like many of the top ulama, he was an ambitious man, and saw in Qom an opportunity to improve his status.

Under his direction Qom became one of the most prominent centers of Shi'ite education in Iran and throughout the Muslim world. Borujerdi remained the head of the Faiziyeh for more than 15 years.

Like Ha'eri before him, Borujerdi had experienced

the trying events of the Constitutional Revolution, which had divided the ulama. The division was caused by the disagreement over whether the ulama should be involved in political movements. Some opposition to the activist ulama also existed within the general Iranian population.

During the 1950s Borujerdi refused to allow his students to be politically active, and he himself kept quiet on such issues. Borujerdi reserved his criticism for those ulama who took part in politics, and sometimes exiled them from Qom.

Through these years, up to the early 1960s, Khomeini quietly followed Borujerdi's lead. There is no record of Khomeini participating in political matters. Khomeini tried not to offend Borujerdi or other leading ulama. He also did not want to damage his standing in the community.

Though he did not speak out in public, in his classes Khomeini often commented on government decisions and political events he felt were important. He spoke of the need to support the downtrodden of society and to oppose — if only in

Iranian workers assemble vehicles during World War II. Iran and the nearby Persian Gulf were strategically important to the Allies. The area was a vital route in transporting needed supplies to the Soviet Union, which Hitler's Germany invaded unsuccessfully in 1941.

The 19-year-old Mohammed Reza Pahlavi, Reza Shah's son, salutes before going to Cairo, Egypt, to marry Princess Fawzia, sister of King Farouk of Saudi Arabia. When Reza Shah, who admired German dictator Adolf Hitler, was forced to abdicate by the Allied powers during World War II, his son succeeded him. Khomeini would be his bitter opponent.

words — unjust rule by the state. Similar statements were made in his writings as well.

While still a teacher in the 1950s, Khomeini wrote a number of works, all in the area of law. One was a two-volume work, and another a five-volume book on commercial law. For most readers, including the state censors, these were highly technical, nonpolitical works. However, for those who read carefully, it was clear that Khomeini's ideas were becoming political. In these works, for example, he warned against assisting evil rulers in any way, and he discussed how to resist corrupt governments and how to help the poor. He also took the first significant steps toward formulating his ideas on the relation between the ulama and government. He began to sketch out the idea that since the leading ulama are the ones who know Islam best, they should determine how the government is to be run.

The period of Khomeini's residence in Qom, as a student and then as a teacher, coincided with the reign of Reza Shah, the founder of the Pahlavi dynasty. (His son, Mohammed Reza Pahlavi, would later succeed to the throne.) Reza Shah came to power in 1925 after overthrowing the last of the Qajar rulers. A crude, rough, and often ill-mannered officer before his rise to power, he maintained this style throughout his reign. To show that he was never to be disobeyed, Reza Shah once had a donkey shot to death while local peasants were forced to stand by and watch. The donkey had trespassed on a meadow belonging to Reza Shah.

In 1934 Reza Shah changed his country's name from Persia to Iran. Once in power, Reza Shah was determined to build Iran into a modern, Western-style nation. In his view, one of the main barriers to achieving this goal was the ulama. He set out to undermine their power and standing. Reza Shah established secular courts, with new European-style legal codes. He decreed a number of measures aimed at breaking the hold of the ulama over the educational system. He also tried to interfere in the administration of the vakf, the religious institution the ulama depended on for much of their income. These decisions were made without any attempt to negotiate with the ulama, and were carried out in Reza Shah's dictatorial manner.

These developments greatly disturbed the religious community. Peaceful protests were followed on occasion by open resistance on the part of leading ulama. These were met with beatings and ar-

The Shah of Iran and his second wife, Queen Soraya, visit a peasant family in a small Iranian village in the 1950s. The Shah, whom Khomeini accused of neglecting the poor, continued Reza Shah's modernization program. In 1962 he launched the "White Revolution," which was meant to establish an industrial economy and his own absolute rule.

rests. Many mullahs were jailed. One such incident would later be cited by Khomeini in his sermons. In 1935, in the shrine of Ali al-Rida in Mashhad, a group of ulama were leading a prayer meeting in protest against the policies of Reza Shah. Troops were ordered in. Dozens of people were killed and many hundreds wounded.

Events such as these left a great impression on Khomeini. He often referred to them in his declarations and writings. Nevertheless, it appears that he tried to remain outside the political arena.

During World War II, under pressure from the Allied powers, Reza Shah abdicated. His son, Mohammed Reza Shah Pahlavi, succeeded him. At first, because of the very unstable situation in Iran during and after the war, the new shah was unable to rule with a strong hand.

In 1941, shortly after Reza Shah was removed from office, Khomeini wrote a book called *Kashf al-Asrar*, or *The Unveiling of the Secrets*. In this book he attacked Reza Shah and his circle of advisers. He criticized Reza Shah's cruelty and his dictatorial reign. He questioned the Shah's fitness to rule. He also called on the ulama to take more responsibility in political affairs.

Khomeini did not yet say in this book that the ulama should play a dominant role in political matters. He said they should accept a secondary position behind the ruler; they should work with the state despite its corruption. His view was that the ulama had to help the state in ensuring social and political order because this was to the benefit of the ulama. In return, the state should then support the religious community and help protect its interests. This was Khomeini's main criticism of Reza Shah. He felt the ruler had not supported the ulama and, in fact, had worked to weaken them. He did not, however, call Reza Shah illegitimate, as he would later call his son.

In the 1950s Khomeini became convinced that the only way for Iran to be ruled justly and honestly was for the ulama to take an active part in government. His ideas continued to develop along these lines through the 1960s, when he would go into exile.

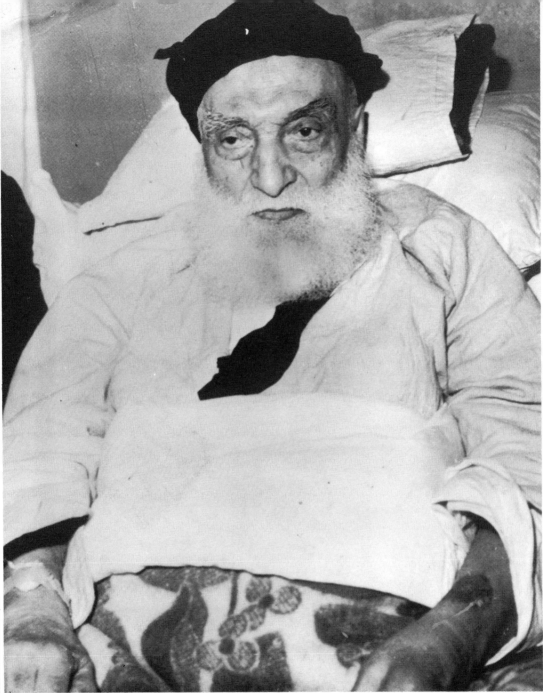

Until his death in 1961, Mohammad Husayn Borujerdi
was head of Iran's Shi'ite community. While Khomeini
was a teacher at the Faiziyeh school in Qom, Borujerdi
succeeded Ha'eri as its director. A "model to be imitated," Borujerdi forbade political activity among his
students, and Khomeini dutifully kept silent — except
in his writings.

5

The Idol Smasher

The event considered the prelude to Khomeini's rise to power occurred in March 1961. In that month, Ayatollah Borujerdi, the head of the Shi'ite ulama community and the only remaining marja'-i taqlid, died. As long as Borujerdi still lived, Khomeini revealed his political ideas only to a few students and occasionally in his writings. With the older man gone, however, he was free to choose his own way.

In 1962 Khomeini was a name known only in the scholarly circles of Qom. He began to earn a reputation for being outspoken and independent in his thinking. He was also considered by many to be somewhat unconventional. He was often reserved, if not unfriendly. He spent much time alone or with only a few students and close family members. He was also known to be ambitious.

With Borujerdi's death the Shi'ite community was left without a recognized leader. A small number of top mujtahids were present in Iran and in the important Shi'ite centers of Iraq. None of these had yet emerged as the new marja'-i taqlid in Borujerdi's place. Since Khomeini had not then become a major

There is no room for play in Islam. . . . It is deadly serious about everything.
—AYATOLLAH KHOMEINI

Mohammed Reza Shah Pahlavi (seen here as he appeared in 1954) succeeded his father, Reza Shah, as Iran's ruling monarch in 1941. After World War II the Shah sought absolute power. He aimed to use Iran's vast oil resources and United States support to turn Iran into a technological "Great Civilization."

figure, he probably knew he would not be a candidate. Despite this, he awaited the opportunity to act. In 1962 that opportunity presented itself.

The year 1962 marked the beginning of the Shah's "Shah-People Revolution," or the "White Revolution." To Khomeini, the Shah's new policies were only an updated version of those of Reza Shah's. In October of that year the Shah's government put into effect a law allowing for the election of local representative councils. What outraged Khomeini and other ulama were the provisions of this new law. First, it allowed women to vote in these elections. To the ulama this meant that specific Islamic principles concerning the conduct of women would be violated. Khomeini issued a statement that the law was an attempt by the government to "corrupt our chaste women."

Second, though the law stated that those elected to office would be sworn in "on the holy book," it did not specifically mention the Koran. To the ulama this meant non-Muslims as well as Muslims could hold office. The ulama argued that by passing this law the government was downplaying the importance of religion while strengthening the political influence of non-Muslim groups. Both were unacceptable. In particular, the ulama were concerned with any increase in the power of the Baha'is, a religious group the ulama condemned.

Most ulama were content with protesting only this specific election law, but Khomeini pushed much further on this issue. He used these protests as an excuse for an extended criticism of the Shah. He denounced the state of the economy, which kept many Iranians poor. He insisted that the law was proof that the Baha'is were working hand-in-hand with agents from Israel to undermine the Muslim faith in Iran. Khomeini himself probably did not believe this was true. Nevertheless, he sensed such claims would win the support of large parts of the population. As later events would show, his instincts were correct. Faced with massive protests, the state canceled the new law.

Even after the law on local councils was abolished Khomeini kept up his criticism of the Shah. He felt sure that he could win wider support this way.

On March 21, 1963, on the eve of Nawruz, the Iranian New Year, Khomeini accused the Iranian state of plotting with the United States and Israel to destroy Islam. He attacked the poverty that gripped the rural areas and the corruption that prevailed in government. By now the Shah and his aides were furious with this upstart from Qom, and they ordered the military to act.

March 22 was the anniversary of the death of the Sixth Imam, Ja'far al-Sadiq, who died in 765. He is said to have been poisoned by the Muslim ruler of the period. The Twelver Shi'a consider al-Sadiq to be not only an Imam but also a martyr. To the Shi'a, his death at the hands of the ruling power also demonstrates how brutal and unjust governments can be. The anniversary is a time when political feelings are likely to reach explosive intensity in Iran. Knowing this, Khomeini used this symbolic occasion as a time to speak out.

Army commandos and members of SAVAK, the feared State Security and Intelligence Organization,

The Shah announces a step in his land reform program in 1955, shortly after his rule had been threatened by Prime Minister Muhammad Mossadeq. In the 1950s the United States made a policy of supporting the Shah. Khomeini and other ulama denounced the Shah's six-point political, legal, and economic reforms as anti-Islamic and unacceptable.

Surrounded by uniformed Iranian police, three men arrested for publishing communist literature are photographed as they and their printing press are driven to jail. Under the Shah, the military and the state security agency (SAVAK), both trained and supplied by the United States and Israel, were used increasingly to enforce repressive policies. During the Shah's reign, tens of thousands of civilians were killed or tortured by SAVAK and the military.

stormed the Faiziyeh school that day. They ransacked the school, beat up dozens of students, and even pushed some of them off roofs and balconies. They succeeded in killing one of the students, as well as injuring many others. They arrested Khomeini and several other ulama, although all of them were released after a short detention. This too worked to Khomeini's advantage.

He had already denounced the Shah and his government as corrupt, dictatorial, and unfit to rule. What better evidence of this than an attack on a school? He continued to agitate against the Shah using this attack as ammunition. By now Khomeini was attracting a great deal of attention outside of Qom. His name was mentioned frequently, his sermons attacking the Shah were quoted over and

over, and, with the assault on the Faiziyeh, all eyes were turned towards Qom. For many of the talebehs within Qom itself, it appeared their wishes for a new political leader were coming true.

In June 1963, a few months after the Faiziyeh incident, Khomeini made the speech that would fully establish his reputation. This was the Muslim month of Muharram, and that year June 3 coincided with Ashurah. Ashurah is celebrated throughout the Shi'ite Muslim world as the anniversary of the murder of Husayn by Yazid at Karbala. It is marked by a number of events, including processions and a special theatrical performance called *ta'ziyeh*. Ashurah has traditionally been a time when political and religious emotions run high.

Even Khomeini's followers would be surprised by Khomeini's vehemence. Loudspeakers were set up both within the school and outside as well, so the huge crowd that had assembled could hear Khomeini. A portable generator was brought to the Faiziyeh in case SAVAK agents in Qom cut off the electricity. A few of Khomeini's students came prepared to record the sermon in order to have copies made later for distribution.

Khomeini showed how politically astute he was. He had chosen a day when, traditionally, most Iranians are encouraged to think about Husayn, Yazid, and the powerfully symbolic events at Karbala. Feelings were running against the Shah among large sectors of the Iranian population. Khomeini appealed to all these sentiments at once. He not only stressed the unjust suffering experienced by Husayn at Yazid's hands, he made a direct connection between Husayn's suffering and the injustices present in modern-day Iran. He was telling his audience that Yazid, the historic murderer of Husayn, and the Shah were one and the same.

Khomeini arrived in the afternoon surrounded by his students and followers. He settled himself before the microphone and began to speak. Instantly, the electricity was shut off. The emergency generator was hooked up and Khomeini continued:

"It is now the afternoon of Ashurah. Sometimes when I recall the events of Ashurah, a question oc-

> *The Shah is saying that he is granting liberty to the people. Hear me, you pompous toad! Who are you to grant freedom? It is Allah who grants freedom . . . it is Islam which grants freedom.*
> —AYATOLLAH KHOMEINI

UPI/BETTMANN NEWSPHOTOS

Iranian "educational corps- men" are trained in the late 1960s as part of the Shah's secular (nonreligious) liter- acy program. In 1963, after the beginning of the Shah's "White Revolution," SAVAK forces attacked the Faiziyeh religious school in Qom. Khomeini responded to the incident in his famed anti- Shah speech on the holy day of Ashurah.

curs to me: if the regime of Yazid ibn Mu'awiyah wished to make war against Husayn, why did it com- mit such savage and inhuman crimes against the defenseless women and innocent children? What had Husayn's six-month-old infant done? It seems to me that Yazid had a far more basic aim: he was opposed to the very existence of the family of the Prophet.

"A similar question occurs to me now. If the ty- rannical regime of Iran simply wished to oppose the ulama, what business did it have tearing the Qur'an [Koran] to shreds on the day it attacked Fayziyeh Madrasah [Faiziyeh madreseh]? Indeed, what busi- ness did it have with the madrasah or with its stu- dents, like the 18-year-old sayid who was killed? What had he done against the Shah, against the government, against the tyrannical regime? We come to the conclusion that this regime also has a more basic aim: they are fundamentally opposed to Islam itself and the existence of the religious class."

He asserted that the Shah had allied with Israel and other foreign powers in order to wage this war against the mullahs and Islam. Israel, he said, hoped to steal Iran's wealth and to bring Islam to its knees. Khomeini then blasted the Shah with the following words:

"Shah, I don't wish the same to happen to you; I don't want you to become like your father. Listen to my advice, listen to the ulama of Islam. They desire the welfare of the nation, the welfare of the country. Don't listen to Israel; Israel can't do anything for you. You miserable wretch, 45 years of your life have passed; isn't it time for you to think and reflect a little, to learn a lesson from the experience of your father?"

On June 5, two days after this speech, security men broke into Khomeini's house and arrested him. He was taken to Tehran and placed in a military barracks. News of his arrest spread through Iran. Violent demonstrations broke out in Tehran, then Qom, Shiraz, Isfahan, and Mashhad. The Shah called out his troops and the battles that followed were among the bloodiest Iran had seen. Martial (military) law was declared in all the major urban centers. Hundreds were killed, and many others were wounded.

Khomeini was not the only member of the ulama to be arrested, yet only he and two others were kept imprisoned after the situation had calmed. Rumors circulated that the state intended to put Khomeini on trial; others said that the man considered a leading religious figure by many mullahs would be executed. A group of prominent religious leaders, including critics of Khomeini's provocative style, petitioned the government not to put Khomeini on trial. Their petition succeeded.

Khomeini was held by the government for 10 months until April 1964. His supporters within the ulama, many of whom were younger mullahs, worked to have him released. Some from this period became very close to Khomeini.

On his release, the Shah's advisers claimed that

As long as the Shah's satanic power prevails, not a single true representative of the people can possibly be elected.
—AYATOLLAH KHOMEINI

The Shah crowns himself, his wife, Empress Farah Diba, and his son at his lavish coronation on October 16, 1967. He postponed his coronation until his "Shah-People," or "White," social revolution was accomplished. "But now that everyone is happy [in Iran] I allow my coronation to take place," he said.

Khomeini had agreed not to involve himself in politics any longer. Khomeini denied this. To show his ideas had not changed, he gave three more speeches in which he denounced the Shah. He also called for a greater role in government for the ulama, although his ideas on this issue were still not fully developed.

Khomeini had become a major figure on the Iranian political scene. He had won the support of the lower classes by attacking the Shah's economic policies, which had created a widening gap between the rich and poor classes of Iran. Many other Iranians supported Khomeini because he upheld the independence of Iran. The Shah had brought numerous foreign military and economic advisers into Iran, and this made many Iranians apprehensive about their country's future.

Khomeini, up to now, had little backing among the middle classes. They were not sure what to make of him. Although many members of this class were dissatisfied with the Shah's rule, they had benefited somewhat from his economic policies. A continued influx of foreigners into Iran, and the favored treatment they received from the Shah's government, nevertheless caused worry. They also remembered the days of foreign occupation.

Khomeini had continually spoken out against the Shah's strong ties with the United States and Israel. He also distrusted the activities of the foreign military and commercial delegations.

In October 1964 a controversial bill came before the Iranian parliament (or *Majlis*). Handpicked by the Shah's advisers, parliament, it was assumed, would pass the bill. Parliament did approve the bill, but only after many members voted against it or refused to vote at all. Within this body of the Shah's loyal followers, an outcry was raised over the new law's provisions. Called the "status of forces" law, it gave diplomatic immunity to all American military advisers, and to their families and staffs. None of these Americans could be tried in an Iranian court. This, of course, aroused memories of the same privileges given to the European representatives in the 19th century.

Shortly afterward, parliament approved a $200

> *Ideologies of the West must be resisted. They are the forward arm of corruption, the silken curtain behind which hides the greed of graspers and the dreams of the dominators.*
> —HASSAN AL BANA
> founder of the
> Muslim Brotherhood

million loan from the United States. To the opposition it was clear that the Shah had made a humiliating concession to the United States in return for the loan.

Khomeini responded by denouncing the law and all those involved with it. His statement captured the attention of all levels of Iranian society. His comments found their way into a leaflet that was circulated throughout the nation. Cassette recordings were made of Khomeini's sermon and were widely distributed.

As usual, Khomeini's words were blunt: "A few days ago, the bill was taken to the lower house of parliament . . . with a few deputies voicing their opposition, but the bill was passed anyhow. . . . They have reduced the Iranian people to a level lower than that of an American dog. If someone runs over a dog belonging to an American, he will be prosecuted. Even if the Shah himself were to run over a dog belonging to an American, he would be prosecuted. But if an American cook runs over the Shah, the head of state, no one will have the right to interfere with him. Why? Because they wanted a loan and America demanded this in return."

He also attacked the United States. He warned that parliament's actions amounted to treason against Iran and against the Koran. "If the religious leaders have influence, they will not permit this nation to be the slave of Britain one day, and America the next," Khomeini proclaimed.

Within a few days of making this statement, Khomeini was arrested and, this time, banished from Iran — first to Turkey. In October 1965, he was permitted to travel to Najaf, in nearby Iraq.

This time there were no riots following Khomeini's arrest and banishment, probably because the clashes in 1963 had been so bloody. By now the Shah's policies had gained support from some sectors of the population. Khomeini's reputation, however, was greater than ever. His stubborn defense of Islam and of Iran had won him the leadership over many of the ulama, and the support of large numbers of other Iranians. While in exile, he worked ceaselessly to maintain this position.

Young, bikini-clad Western women on a Caspian Sea beach pass a traditionally dressed Iranian Shi'ite woman. Modern Western values, encouraged by the Shah's various reforms, clashed with the Koran's teachings, according to Khomeini. He believed that giving Iranian women the right to vote was a way to "corrupt our chaste women."

6

The Voice of the Exile

Khomeini remained in Najaf for 13 years. This city is the site of the shrine of Ali ibn Abu Talib. It is one of the most holy cities of the Shi'ite Muslim sect. Every year thousands of pilgrims travel there, and for many Shi'a, a pilgrimage to Najaf is almost as important as the pilgrimage to Mecca. Najaf is also one of the most important centers of Shi'ite education. There are several large schools there that have, over the centuries, attracted large numbers of students and scholars.

Khomeini arrived in Najaf in October 1965. He was met by a number of students, many of whom had come from Qom to study with him. He was recognized by now as a leading ayatollah of Iran both for his learning and his outspoken defense of Islam.

For a number of mullahs, Khomeini had become more than a leading member of the Shi'ite community. He was considered to be, in fact, a marja'-i taqlid, a model to be imitated. Mostly because of his political and religious stance, many younger mullahs had chosen him as their model. Unlike his teacher Borujerdi, he was not the only such figure of the period.

If the Shah is not destroyed, you shall all become slaves of pagans. Foreigners shall take your womenfolk; they shall plunder all your natural wealth and put the Muslim community to eternal shame.
—AYATOLLAH KHOMEINI

Ayatollah Khomeini meets with reporters at Neauphle-le-Château, near Paris, France, where he spent four months after being forced to leave Najaf, Iraq, in late 1978. After his famous speech in June 1963, Khomeini's arrest touched off bloody riots throughout Iran. He subsequently spent 13 years in exile in Iraq.

UPI/BETTMANN NEWSPHOTOS

Yet, unlike the Shah's critics in the leading religious circles, Khomeini's position was clear and uncompromising. Khomeini called directly upon the Iranian people to reject the Shah's rule and to overthrow him. During his 14-year exile, the ayatollah pounded away at this simple message.

Cassette recordings of his talks became an important vehicle for the dissemination of his ideas. These tapes were smuggled into Iran, copied, and then distributed.

By exiling Khomeini, the Shah unintentionally gave him even greater opportunity to speak out. The Iranian secret police had less freedom to act in Iraq than in Iran. Thus Khomeini continued to haunt the Shah.

Over the next 14 years the ulama in many places were kept under constant surveillance by SAVAK and the army. SAVAK also infiltrated several religious associations, aiming to weaken them. All religious writings were censored.

As under Reza Shah, mullahs were beaten, jailed, tortured, and sent into exile. A number were also killed. One famous example occurred in 1970, when a top religious leader, Ayatollah Sa'idi, was arrested and tortured to death in prison.

The government also attempted to undermine the ulama in their traditional areas of influence — religion and education. The government set up, for example, several religious schools staffed by state-appointed ulama. The state assumed control over a number of mosques (Muslim houses of worship), and tightened control over the vakf, a major source of the ulama's income.

By 1977 the majority of Iranians clearly had not given up supporting the independent ulama, nor decided to back these new policies. A number of leading religious figures, as well as Khomeini, in exile, came out against the state, which only further alienated the Shah from the Iranian people.

Khomeini, in Najaf, was disturbed by these attacks on the religious community. He saw the new policies as evidence that the Shah was opposed not only to the ulama, but also to Islam. By suppressing the religious leadership, the Shah was relegating the faith to a second-place position in Iran. Khomeini was also convinced that these efforts were carried out to strengthen not only the Shah, but also the influence of foreign powers in Iran.

The Shah was determined to modernize Iran. He called his program for a new technological Iran "the Great Civilization." Unlike his father, however, the Shah possessed enormous oil revenues to draw from, and thus ever-increasing economic ties to the West. With these assets, the Shah set out to transform Iran. The ulama, the Shah was told by his advisers, were the most powerful opponents of this scheme. He would have to repress them.

In a number of sermons Khomeini accused the Shah of being a puppet in the hands of the American and Israeli governments. He pointed to, for example, the foreign businessmen he believed were being allowed to take over the oil industry of Iran in exchange for fancy and unnecessary military technology. By allowing these groups enormous privileges, the Shah was, in Khomeini's eyes, placing the Iranian economy in foreign hands. The ayatollah's concern for the independence of Iran had always existed alongside his concern for the health of Islam.

A political cartoonist's interpretation of the nationalization of the Iranian oil industry in 1951 by the *Majlis* (Iranian parliament), showing "John Bull," symbol of Great Britain, being tossed from the oil field. After Iran took over the British-controlled Anglo-Iranian Oil Company, the United States led a worldwide boycott of Iranian oil.

The Shah's policies, however, were only one focus of Khomeini's interest while in Najaf. Khomeini perceived certain groups as enemies of Iran and Islam. Some included representatives of the United States and Israel working in Iran for their respective governments, providing support for the Shah. Israel, for example, helped the Shah in 1957 to organize SAVAK, which became notorious over the next 20 years for its often ruthless activities. Systematic torture of citizens accused of opposition to the Shah was a specialty of SAVAK. Carried on with the knowledge and perhaps the encouragement of the U.S. government, SAVAK torture sessions injured, maimed, or killed tens of thousands of Iranians during the Shah's reign.

For Khomeini, the United States presented the greatest threat to Islam in the world. Time and again he would point out how supportive the United States was of the Shah. These relations, which were to span 40 years, developed steadily after World War II as a result of American economic and political interests in Iran.

Iran became a major oil producer by the late

Iranian oil production reached 31 million tons in 1950. Iran's industrial development was a goal of Reza Shah and his son. Reza Shah first allowed Great Britain to develop the Iranian oil resources. After World War II, the United States provided arms, advisers, and economic assistance.

1940s. During the war Iran's oil had been vital to the nations fighting the Nazis, and in years afterward Iranian oil production boomed, reaching a total of 31 million tons by 1950. Oil companies based in the United States, along with several British firms, tried very hard to assume a leading role in this industry. The United States government, for its part, was concerned with the Soviet Union's involvement in Iran. To increase its own influence, the United States backed nationalist groups in Iran that opposed the Soviets. Arms sales to Iran were stepped up, and growing numbers of military and economic advisers were sent to assist the Shah's government.

From 1947 to 1948 one group of Americans helped create a large development program. The program was called the Seven Year Plan, with a firm from the United States playing an important role in setting it up. Within two years, little had been accomplished to improve the Iranian economy, but corruption in government had increased.

As dissatisfaction with the economic situation mounted, the Iranian parliament and the American and British companies involved received the blame. One specific target was the huge British company called the Anglo-Iranian Oil Company (AIOC). For many Iranians, these companies cared little for the problems facing Iran, and were simply exploiting the country for their own gain.

This dissatisfaction finally led to a change in government in April 1951, when Muhammad Mossadeq became prime minister of Iran. His election to office coincided with a decision by the parliament to nationalize the oil industry, a move led by Mossadeq himself. This was a popular decision within Iran and brought Mossadeq much support. According to British journalist Robert Graham, Mossadeq's ministry "was a direct challenge to the Shah's authority as monarch — and he [the Shah] came very close to losing." The United States, however, was alarmed by the move and launched a campaign to discredit Mossadeq, portraying him as a religious fanatic bent on attacking the West and its interests. It also helped to set up an effective worldwide boycott of Iranian oil. The cut in oil revenues badly damaged

Iran is a rotten apple, and all we have to do is wait for it to fall into our hands.
—NIKITA KHRUSHCHEV
Soviet leader

the Iranian economy.

Despite the economic situation, Mossadeq remained popular. Relations with the United States became steadily worse. By August 1953, demonstrations were held in Tehran. At first these demonstrations opposed the Shah and supported Mossadeq. On August 16 the Shah fled the country. Mossadeq then sent troops in to restore order. Many of the groups that had backed him withdrew their support. On August 19 another demonstration was held, but this time against Mossadeq, with the support of the army, the Shah, and other powerful groups. Mossadeq's enemies gained the upper hand and were able to have him arrested. His government finally collapsed, and the Shah returned to rule Iran.

The U.S. Central Intelligence Agency (CIA), with British support, had engineered the coup that overthrew the democratically elected Mossadeq and replaced him with the dictatorial regime of the Shah. For large groups of Iranians, including many ulama, such foreign interference was an outrage.

The United States now was the dominant foreign power in Iran. It took over more than 40 percent of the Anglo-Iranian Oil Company, which had regained control of about half of the oil production in Iran.

The high point of the relationship between the United States government and the Shah came in the early 1970s. By this time the Shah had developed almost a mania for modern and complex military equipment. President Richard Nixon and his national security adviser, Henry Kissinger, initiated a new foreign policy in which Iran became a crucial link in the American alliance system in the Middle East. With its military might, Iran could serve as a "policeman" over the Persian Gulf area and its precious oil fields. The United States began to sell Iran large quantities of arms, to the satisfaction of the Shah. Arms shipments from the United States quickly increased Iran's power and influence among its neighbors.

Ironically, after the 1979 revolution, these same arms would serve to strengthen Khomeini's new government. With these weapons, and Iranian troops once loyal to the Shah, Khomeini's regime would be able to maintain its position through several tense years.

Khomeini viewed the United States support differently than did the Shah. By consistently backing the Shah, the United States demonstrated that it was not going to encourage political and economic reform in Iran. The Shah used the new military equipment and advisers from the United States to suppress all internal disagreement with his policies. To his opponents, as well as to many other Iranians, the United States shared responsibility with the Shah for political oppression in Iran.

During his stay in Najaf, Khomeini constantly denounced the United States. He attacked the Shah, calling him a puppet of the real enemy, which he considered to be the United States. In his view, if the Shah was opposing the Islamic religion, it was really the Americans who were urging him to take this stand. Later Khomeini would label the United States "the Great Satan."

Through the late 1960s, and up to 1979, both the Shah and the United States government virtually ignored Khomeini. At one point the Shah referred to him as an "obscure individual."

Khomeini saw enemies of Iran and the Muslim faith not only outside the country but inside it as well. Other targets of his attacks included the wealthy classes of Iran, who imitated Western customs and ideas. They, along with growing political and economic interference by Western nations, were resented by certain sectors of Iran's population — the ulama in particular. In Khomeini's view, these Western-influenced elements were corrupt. They also helped the Shah's government in its policies against the ulama and the Muslim faith.

Another group targeted by Khomeini for his typically vehement criticism was the Baha'is. A 19th-century offshoot of Islam, the Baha'i faith is considered heretical by Muslims, especially by the Twelver Shi'a. Throughout the 19th and 20th centuries the Baha'is constantly met with antagonism from the ulama. In the 1960s and 1970s Khomeini singled them out as participants in the activities of the Shah's secret police and as agents of Israel and the

Muhammad Mossadeq on trial in 1953. Mossadeq became prime minister of Iran in 1951, when the Iranian parliament took the oil industry out of foreign hands. Iranians — including many Shi'ite leaders — blamed U.S. and British companies for economic woes. When Mossadeq challenged the Shah's rule, the United States helped engineer Mossadeq's downfall.

UPI/BETTMANN NEWSPHOTOS

United States. After the 1979 revolution he would act harshly against the Baha'is.

In his early years as a dissident, Khomeini attacked first Reza Shah, then his son. Never before, however, had he openly attacked Iran's monarchical system of government. His criticisms were aimed at those who occupied the office, and not the office itself. By the late 1960s, however, Khomeini's view had changed. It was in this period that Khomeini began to criticize not only the Shah but also his system of government.

By 1969 Khomeini's ideas on government and the role of Islam had become fully developed. The core of these ideas came from lectures Khomeini gave in Iraq. In early 1970, a series of these lectures was recorded and transcribed by one of Khomeini's pupils. These lectures were compiled and published under the title *Velayet-e Faqih: Hukumat-e Eslami* (*The Governance of the Jurist: Islamic Government*). This work has been translated into Arabic, Turkish, Urdu, French, and English. It is probably Khomeini's best-known work.

In this book, Khomeini condemns monarchical forms of government. He states that Islam "proclaims monarchy and hereditary succession wrong and invalid." To support this position, Khomeini cites the prophet Muhammad, who is believed to have written letters to monarchs ruling in areas neighboring Arabia, calling on them to accept Islam and to change their form of government.

Khomeini's second point is that as believers in Islam, the Iranian people are obliged by their faith

Armored vehicles parade through Tehran in 1975. The Shah's regime, whose foreign currency reserves reached $26 billion in the late 1970s, poured vast amounts of money into arms purchases from the United States. After the Iranian Revolution these stockpiled weapons would be used by the new "Islamic Government," as Khomeini called it.

AP/WIDE WORLD

to overthrow oppressive governments. Such rulers must be overthrown and, in Khomeini's view, it is the duty of the Muslim community to do so. Khomeini's real target was, of course, the Shah. Khomeini also attacked what he saw as corruption in government, immorality, Westernization, and secularization (the replacement of religious values with nonreligious ones). Khomeini believed the Shah helped introduce these ills into Iranian society.

Such corrupt forms of government, Khomeini states, must be replaced by a government based upon Islam. Such a state would be based on the teachings of the Koran and Sunnah and would be modeled after the early Muslim community headed by Muhammad in the 7th century. Khomeini argues this is not only the ideal form of government, it is also one that is realizable in this century.

As the title implies, the most important part of the book concerns the leadership of this Islamic state. He had encouraged the mullahs to show increased concern for social and political issues. Never before had Khomeini gone so far as to demand that the mullahs take a dominant role in politics and government. His views began to change after his banishment from Iran. By the late 1960s he began to say that the only acceptable leaders for the Islamic state were the ulama.

Islam, for Khomeini, provides guidelines not only for the religious life of the community, but also for its social and political life. Such a state would require a group of people who could interpret and apply the law to the everyday problems of government and society. Those who know this law best, of course, are the leaders of the ulama — the mujtahids and the "models." Such men are also known by the term *fuqaha* (the plural of *faqih*), a man thoroughly versed in Islamic law.

In Khomeini's view, such a person has the two qualities needed in a ruler of an Islamic state: a sense of justice and knowledge of the law. Such a man's religious and legal training allows him to make just decisions with respect to all issues confronting society. At any one time there exists only a small number of such jurists, or legal experts. Only

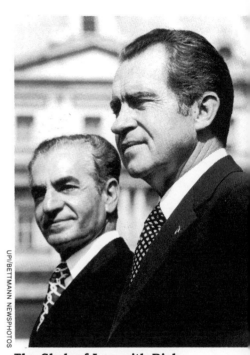

UPI/BETTMANN NEWSPHOTOS

The Shah of Iran with Richard Nixon, president of the United States, in 1973. Calling the Shah "a world statesman of the first rank," Nixon believed that Iran would be the "policeman" of the Persian Gulf region. Khomeini called the Shah a puppet of the United States.

they, according to Khomeini, can serve as the rightful leaders of the community. The individual in this group who possesses these two qualities in the highest degree should be given complete authority.

In fact, Khomeini was discussing what should occur in the absence of the Hidden Imam, still considered the ultimate source of legitimate leadership for the community. Since the Twelfth Imam was still in hiding, however, it was necessary to turn to another source of leadership.

Copies of Khomeini's book were smuggled into Iran by the thousands and widely distributed. Khomeini's writings began to win him a wider following. It was now clear that a war was brewing between Khomeini and the Shah. Khomeini called the Shah unfit to rule, and again declared that it was the duty of the Iranian people to overthrow him.

Khomeini's verbal attacks on the Shah continued through the early 1970s. In 1971 the Shah held a lavish banquet to celebrate what he called "2,500 years of Iranian kingship." Held at Persepolis, an ancient capital of Persia, it was a hugely expensive event, attended by leaders from all over the world. For Khomeini, concerned as always with corruption and the plight of the poor, the banquet was an outrageous extravagance. It was only an additional illustration of how unfit the Shah was to rule.

Although they refused to publicly acknowledge it,

Iranian citizens display photographs of relatives who died, they charge, at the hands of the Shah's SAVAK torturers. During his exile in Iraq, Khomeini's messages were smuggled into Iran on cassette recordings. He called upon the people to overthrow the Shah, whose government relied increasingly on violent repression.

AP/WIDE WORLD

the Shah and his advisers were growing concerned with Khomeini's ideas and popularity. Surveillance by SAVAK agents was stepped up, as was harassment of Khomeini's supporters within Iran. The state took two additional steps that were not only more serious but, ironically, served to fuel opposition to the Shah.

In October 1977 Khomeini's eldest son, Mostafa, died at the Muslim shrine at Karbala, Iraq. The circumstances surrounding his death remain mysterious. It is widely believed, however, that he was killed, possibly poisoned, by SAVAK agents. Over the next few days demonstrations were held in protest of the alleged killing and in support of Ayatollah Khomeini.

In January 1978 the leading semiofficial newspaper, *Ittila'at*, printed an article that accused Khomeini of being an "adventurer," a man without faith, and an agent of foreign powers. These and other attacks on Khomeini met with immediate reactions in Iran. In Qom, groups of religious students took to the streets and clashed with the police. Many of the students were killed and wounded. Demonstrations also occurred in other parts of Iran.

Those killed were mourned as martyrs for the traditional period of 40 days, then another demonstration was held. On February 18, 40 days after the Qom massacre, a number of people were shot

Iranians carry the casket of a demonstrator killed in a clash with the Shah's army in 1978. As Khomeini's followers became more determined to overthrow the Shah, riots flared up in the Iranian cities of Qom, Tabriz, and Yazd. Khomeini told his supporters to appeal "to the soldiers' hearts," and urged the troops to desert the army.

in a riot in Tabriz. Forty days after that, approximately 100 people were killed by troops in a demonstration in the city of Yazd.

Khomeini was convinced that the largest obstacle facing the revolution was the army. Confident that the huge crowds of his followers could counter the Shah's military forces, he told the army not to kill their fellow Muslims. As for his supporters, he told them to "appeal to the soldiers' hearts even if they fire on you and kill you." In his taped sermons, he directed the army to abandon the Shah. They were the soldiers of God, he declared; they must not fight for the tyrant (*taghut*) who rebels against Allah.

Khomeini's most important strategy against the monarch was to discredit the Shah personally. The spirit of this campaign was summed up in the slogan "Death to the Shah." He accused the Shah of insatiable greed, betrayal of Islam, and perversion. Khomeini concentrated on depicting the struggle as one of life and death between the Shah on one side and the Iranian people and Islam on the other. His messages called the Shah "the American snake whose head must be smashed with a stone."

Opposition to the Shah was now widespread. In response, the Shah tried several new measures, all of them futile. The Shah then pressured the Iraqi government to either silence Khomeini, who continued to make statements to his Iranian followers, or to banish him. Khomeini refused to be muzzled and was finally asked to leave Iraq.

Khomeini (center) leads a morning prayer at Neauphle-le-Château, France, where he took up residence in October 1978 after his banishment from Iraq. Excellent communications and transportation between France and Iran enabled supporters to meet with him; Khomeini's access to the Western news media allowed him to give 120 interviews in four months.

After being refused entry at the Kuwaiti border, he considered going to Syria. But Ibrahim Yazdi, later a close adviser to Khomeini, urged him to go to France. Khomeini reluctantly agreed. In October 1978 he flew to Paris and established his headquarters in the suburban village of Neauphle-le-Château. Although France was further from Iran than Iraq, this decision proved beneficial to Khomeini's movement for two reasons.

Journalists from leading newspapers, magazines, and television flocked to the Parisian suburb to interview Khomeini. He quickly realized the value of this publicity and took advantage of it. During the four months he remained in France, Khomeini gave more than 120 interviews. Such exposure not only increased worldwide sympathy for the Shah's opponents, it also encouraged the groups working against the state within Iran.

Communication links and transportation between Iran and France were excellent. Khomeini had ready access to the Iranian people. His statements were phoned in daily to Tehran or Qom, recorded, written down, and then copies were distributed. His supporters were able to fly directly to Paris and confer with Khomeini. Meanwhile, demonstrations and riots became regular occurrences. Calls for the Shah's abdication were pouring in from all over Iran.

Khomeini is shown a newspaper headline of January 16, 1979, that reads: "The Shah Is Leaving." While Khomeini was in France with his advisers, including future high officials Abolhasan Bani Sadr and Ibrahim Yazdi, support for the Shah in Iran dwindled. Asked in December 1978 if the revolution would succeed, he answered, "I have confidence in God."

79

7

The Reckoning

In January 1979, after withdrawing huge sums of money from the royal family's banks, Mohammed Reza Pahlavi fled Iran. Fifteen days later, on January 31, 1979, Khomeini returned to his country in triumph. Reporters in Tehran estimated that more than 2 million people were on hand to welcome him. Over the course of the previous months he had gained the support of nearly all the opposition groups within the country and his popularity seemed overwhelming.

Like many history-making figures before him, Khomeini has become the focus of countless legends that are often false, or only partly based on fact. According to one such story, in the spring of 1979, after Khomeini's return to Iran, a 50-man delegation from Khomein came to Qom, bringing gifts and an invitation. The delegation's leader went before the ayatollah and said, "Visit your people, O smasher of idols." Khomeini was probably the only famous son ever to come from their small village. His visitors were anxious that he agree to travel to Khomein for a brief stay. Khomeini, unsmiling and aloof, paused for only an instant, then replied curtly,

If he were a man of greater stature, a human being displaying a greater degree of self-awareness, he might well have been a tragic figure.
—DAVID H. ALBERT
American historian, on
Mohammed Reza Shah Pahlavi

Khomeini arrives in Tehran, Iran, from exile in France, on January 31, 1979. The Shah had abdicated and fled Iran. Sometimes called the Great *Faqih*, or jurist, Khomeini wrote *The Governance of the Jurist: Islamic Government*. In this book he claims that Islam regards "monarchy . . . as wrong and invalid."

Soldiers of the Shah's army hold portraits of Khomeini while demonstrating their support for the new Islamic regime. In 1963 the army reacted harshly to Shi'ite demonstrations that followed Khomeini's arrest. By 1978 some soldiers had joined the revolutionaries.

"No, there will be no visit." The delegation withdrew, and the question was probably never raised again.

The story indicates several things about Khomeini. That Khomein sent such a large delegation to him shows Khomeini's standing in Iran just after the revolution. In 1979 he received hundreds of such delegations from all parts of Iran. These groups came to show their respect and to demonstrate their support of him.

This story also illustrates the coldness of Khomeini's manner, a feature of his personality recognized earlier at the Faiziyeh by the other teachers. Journalists who met Khomeini following the revolution of 1979 also noticed this characteristic. His aloofness was intimidating to many, but to others, it was reason enough to dislike him.

"Smasher of Idols" was one of a number of phrases that referred to Khomeini at this time. Such phrases were used as praise or, as with the Khomein delegation, out of respect.

Khomeini's triumphant return to Iran and the Shah's own self-imposed exile capped a long and complex series of events. In Khomeini's absence from Iran, the Shah had launched programs of economic expansion and increased political repression. Thus began the process that doomed the Shah's rule and brought Khomeini to power.

Khomeini's standing had developed during the 14 years he was absent from Iran. From the early 1960s his words and deeds had gained more and more attention, first in Qom, then throughout the country. Through this period, the Shah's rule grew increasingly oppressive and unpopular. Khomeini's uncompromising views on the Shah and his regime

Are you not aware of the crimes that have been committed here? Are you not aware that they have plundered the wealth of this country? And that they have left behind a hungry nation? Do you not know that they subjected this nation to oppression and torture over a period of 50 years and robbed her whole wealth to pay the big powers?

—AYATOLLAH KHOMEINI
to a group of foreign
clergymen, on the
Pahlavi dynasty

therefore grew increasingly persuasive as the years went on.

Sixteen years after Mossadeq threatened the Shah's rule in 1953, the Iranian economy experienced nearly constant growth. This was due primarily to the huge amounts of oil Iran produced, the oil boom reaching its peak in 1973. Rising industrial production and a greater role in world trade also contributed to this growth. In addition, the Shah carried out reform programs in land distribution, agricultural production, and education.

The Shah and his advisers either worsened old problems or created new ones. Gradually these came to outweigh the benefits of economic growth and the limited reforms, and led, finally, to the end of the Pahlavi dynasty.

The first problem was the Shah's leadership. As the years went on, the Shah grew increasingly arbitrary in his decisions. Rather than wait for approval from parliament, he often made policy by imperial decree, thus appearing to be the tyrant Khomeini accused him of being. His subordinates behaved similarly. In the mid-1970s, for example, in order to make way for new streets and avenues,

Merchants and customers in a traditional Iranian marketplace. Although Iran's oil industry created tremendous wealth, the *bazaaris* — the shopkeepers, artisans, and small manufacturers — became distrustful of the Shah's economic policies. The bazaaris, whose sons frequently joined the Shi'ite ulama, gave significant support to Khomeini.

EASTFOTO CNA

the mayor of Tehran ordered certain residential neighborhoods bulldozed, thus setting off riots.

Demanding total authority, the Shah suppressed all independent political parties, the press, and many labor unions. He filled parliament with his supporters. State control was imposed on universities, schools, business groups, and religious organizations. Near the end of his reign, he turned more often to the army and secret police to crush those who opposed him.

As their political freedoms were denied, many groups — including the ulama — became more and more radical. After the army's harsh reaction to the 1963 demonstrations and SAVAK's ruthless tactics drove many to take more radical positions, several groups emerged that chose armed struggle as their response to the Shah's policies.

Iran's economic problems played into the hands of the Shah's opponents. Although the Iranian economy prospered in the late 1960s and early 1970s, the benefits were unevenly distributed. The gap between rich and poor widened considerably. While the small upper class grew more wealthy, the lower classes found themselves hard-pressed. Furthermore, cities and towns, rather than rural areas, benefited most from the Shah's economic policies. "The Shah," writes Polish journalist Ryszard Kapuściński, "got drunk on visions of atomic power plants, computerized production lines, and large-scale petrochemical complexes."

When oil prices skyrocketed in 1974, serious upheavals took place both economically and socially in Iran. Within a year or two, oil revenues leaped from $5 billion to $20 billion a year.

Under the Shah, Iran's foreign currency reserves totaled roughly $26 billion in the late 1970s. The Shah's army was one of the largest in the world and featured some of the finest military technology available. His security and intelligence services were large and well trained.

The Shah's government began vast spending programs. These served to increase inflation and government corruption. People from rural areas began to flock to the cities in search of work, thus creating

In near-freezing temperatures, an Iranian beggar-woman huddles with her child in a Tehran street in January 1979. While the Shah's economic policies were aimed at creating a technological society, Iran's poor suffered due to severe economic inequities, and they grew increasingly loyal to Khomeini during the late 1970s.

AP/WIDE WORLD

large urban slums. Foreign workers and advisers flooded into Iran, which raised unemployment among Iranian workers and added to rising tension.

Apart from Khomeini, there were several political organizations that opposed the Shah, such as the Tudeh (communist) party, which had been formed during 1941 and 1942. It had close ties with the Soviet Union and, later, with the People's Republic of China. Suppressed in 1953 for its tentative support of Mossadeq and for criticizing Western involvement in Iran, the Tudeh continued to oppose the Shah into the 1970s. But ties to the Soviet Union and to China alienated the party from other radical groups.

Another was the National Front (NF), a coalition of smaller parties. The NF remained on the scene despite the Shah's suppression of it after 1963, using harassment and arrest against its membership. The National Front contributed to the leadership of the Islamic Revolution in 1979. However, for many of its younger members, the National Front was not radical enough.

The Feda'iyan-e Khalq was one of the organizations started by those radicals for whom the NF was too moderate. The Feda'iyan-e emerged in 1971 when three militant student groups originally formed in the early 1960s came together under one program. The members of the Feda'iyan-e were mostly the children of modern, middle-class Iranian families. As university students, they were frustrated with the repressive policies of the Shah. Starting in February 1971, with an attack on a police station, they began to wage guerrilla warfare against the Shah as well as American military advisers in Iran. Though many of its members were killed or captured, the Feda'iyan-e remained active up to the 1979 revolution.

Larger than the Feda'iyan-e, the Mojahedin-e Khalq was formed by university students in the 1960s. These students were mostly from more traditional urban middle-class families that included many merchants and religious men. The Mojahedin mixed its revolutionary anti-imperialism (opposition to foreign domination) with religious principles

Militants of the Feda'iyan-e Khalq attend a rally of about 50,000 people in 1979. The Feda'iyan-e, a nonreligious radical organization composed primarily of university students from middle-class backgrounds, supported Khomeini's efforts to overthrow the Shah.

AP/WIDE WORLD

Appointed prime minister by the Shah in an eleventh-hour attempt to appease opposition forces, Dr. Shapur Bakhtiyar (flanked by picture of former Prime Minister Mossadeq) had been opposed to the Shah. As violence flared and troops deserted the army, Bakhtiyar advised the Shah to leave Iran. After Khomeini took power, Bakhtiyar also fled.

drawn from modern Islamic doctrines. Though divided into two factions in 1975, the Mojahedin continued to struggle against the Shah. In battles with security forces the Mojahedin suffered many losses, and many of its members were arrested. It nevertheless continued its efforts through 1979.

There were two other leading figures who gained extensive support among the ulama. Ayatollah Mahmud Taleqani was a popular leader based in Tehran. Since the 1950s he had been one of the most important political theoreticians among the ulama working against the Shah. His connections to the Mojahedin, as well as his opinions, caused Taleqani to be jailed. He attracted a great deal of support from leftists and student groups, and played an important role in the 1979 revolution as a mediator between revolutionary groups such as the National Front and the religious groups. Because he was isolated from most ulama, he never commanded the widespread support Khomeini did. Taleqani died in September 1979.

The other figure, Ayatollah Kazem Shariatmadari, had been a student with Khomeini in Qom and later taught there under Borujerdi. His support came from the provinces of Azerbaijan and Khorasan. In 1963 and 1964 he was one of the ulama who petitioned the state not to put Khomeini on trial. Unlike Khomeini, Shariatmadari was moderate in his viewpoint. Thus, during the Islamic Revolution, he kept a distance from many of Khomeini's ideas. He remained popular among moderate and traditional groups during the revolution, but since he did not fully support Khomeini's ideas, tension developed between him and Khomeini's radical followers.

Nevertheless, by 1979 the National Front, the Tudeh, the guerrilla factions, and the ulama united behind a revolution headed by Khomeini. All these organizations gave a share of support to the ayatollah. His sermon at the Faiziyeh on Ashurah in 1963 showed Khomeini chose the language of his statements carefully so as to appeal to as wide an audience as possible. His language was direct and emotional. It was also laden with references to the religious figures Husayn and Yazid that any Iranian could understand. In winning the support of the lower classes in particular, his use of language was important.

In the prerevolutionary period from 1977 to 1979, the urban poor contributed the greatest numbers to demonstrations against the state. Khomeini, who had always championed the cause of the poor, commanded the immense loyalty of *mustazafin*, a word that refers to the the oppressed and deprived. The impoverished classes suffered the most severe hardships under the Shah. Thus, they responded very quickly to Khomeini's attacks on the regime.

Another segment of the Iranian economy that gave Khomeini its support was made up of various urban groups known as *bazaaris*, or workers in small factories, shopkeepers, artisans, and merchants. Their common feature at this time was their

Iran is an oasis of stability in a sea of trouble, and I am sure that the reason for this is the just, the great, and the inspired leadership of your majesty.
—JIMMY CARTER
American president
(1977–1981), addressing
Reza Shah Pahlavi in 1977

AP/WIDE WORLD

The Shah and Empress Farah leave Iran for the last time on January 16, 1979. Rioters had chanted, "Death to the Shah," in Abadan in August 1978 after a movie theater was set ablaze — supposedly by SAVAK — killing more than 400 people. In December millions of demonstrators throughout Iran had demanded the Shah's immediate abdication.

87

A statue of the Shah is wrecked by demonstrators on the day of his departure from Iran. The triumphant revolutionaries destroyed many monuments to the Shah following his abdication in January 1979.

AP/WIDE WORLD

distrust of the policies of the Shah, particularly Westernization and the development of large-scale industry. Also it was common for the sons of bazaaris to become members of the ulama.

Throughout his years in exile a network of supporters within the ulama represented Khomeini and carried out a number of tasks for him. These mullahs cultivated local support, organized demonstrations, propagated Khomeini's ideas, and collected donations. Several prominent leaders of the network were Khomeini's students in earlier days and many would serve in the revolutionary government after 1979. Among them were Morteza Motahari, Muhammad Beheshti, Muhammad Bahonar, and Ali Khamenei. Some, like Beheshti and Motahari, were on good terms with the Shah's government through the early 1970s. Others, like Ali Khamene'i, were more radical and were constantly harassed by SAVAK.

Khomeini's cause gathered momentum through angry protests spun off by the bloody demonstrations in Qom in January 1978. In August over 400 people died in a fire in a movie theater in Abadan. Many Iranians were convinced it had been set by SAVAK agents. This led to further rioting. On September 7, a day known as "Black Friday," troops opened fire on demonstrators who charged them in Jaleh Square in Tehran, killing several hundred people. Strikes by bank employees and civil servants followed in the wake.

Now ill with cancer, the Shah tried two conflicting policies at once. On the one hand, he tried to placate the opposition by appointing popular politicians to office, promising reforms, and arresting unpopular figures, including a former prime minister and a former head of SAVAK. He also launched a campaign of violence against the Baha'i community.

On the other hand, he called frequently on the police and the army to quell the protests directed at his regime. Not only did this lead to increased violence, and larger numbers of dead and wounded, it also began to backfire as many soldiers refused to shoot at the crowds, or simply took their weapons and joined the opposition. This only encouraged the opposition and hastened the Shah's downfall.

December 1978 coincided with the Muslim month of Muharram. By now the regime was on the brink of collapse. On December 11, the day of Ashurah, more than a million people marched in Tehran alone. Violence was rampant and there were desertions from the army. On December 29, Dr. Shapur Bakhtiyar was named prime minister. He had long been an opponent of the Shah, and the Shah hoped this appointment would appease the opposition. It did not. On January 16 the Shah was persuaded by Bakhtiyar to leave Iran for a "vacation" of indefinite length. Eleven days after Khomeini's return to Iran, Bakhtiyar himself fled the country. The overthrow of the regime was complete and Khomeini was now the new ruler of Iran.

With portraits of Khomeini nearby, revolutionary gunmen guard the *Majlis*, the Iranian parliament. Khomeini insisted that the Iranian people, as believers in Islam, were required to rise up against illegitimate and oppressive governments and replace them with a government based on the Koran.

8

"The Punisher of the Tyrants"

Once the euphoria of the revolution's success had subsided, it was obvious Khomeini and his supporters faced a number of obstacles to the establishment of the Islamic state. What to do with the other groups in the revolutionary movement was perhaps the most serious question. Khomeini had needed their backing in the fight against the Shah. Now with the Shah no longer in Iran, Khomeini's main task was to secure his position and establish control of the new Islamic state. He had to consolidate his power.

The man Khomeini chose in February 1979 to head the new government was Mehdi Bazargan. A devoutly religious man, and educated as an engineer in France, Bazargan had been politically active since 1941. In the 1960s he was imprisoned for his radical views and his criticism of the Shah. Because he had made the National Front an important political force, despite the Shah's repression, Bazargan gained a substantial following. In 1978 he and his envoys kept in close touch with Khomeini's circle in France, and after these meetings the National

It never entered anyone's head to come out the way Khomeini did — to reject all that scribbling, all those petitions, resolutions, proposals. To stand before the people, and say "The Shah must go!"
—RYSZARD KAPUŚCIŃSKI
Polish journalist

Khomeini, having returned to Iran in triumph 15 days after the Shah's departure, greets enthusiastic followers. Often referred to as "Imam" — a vicar of the Hidden Imam, after whom the Twelver Shi'a are named — Khomeini would oversee all decisions made by officials in the new, postrevolutionary government.

Foreign Minister Ibrahim Yazdi confers with Mehdi Bazargan, who was appointed head of the new government by Khomeini in February 1979. Politically active since 1941 and extremely religious, Bazargan was jailed in the 1970s for his radical beliefs. He organized the National Front to oppose the Shah. Yazdi had advised Khomeini to seek refuge in France upon leaving Iraq.

Front came out in full support of Khomeini.

An important member of Bazargan's government was Ibrahim Yazdi, who had been one of Khomeini's close associates. When the Iraqis forced Khomeini to leave Najaf, Yazdi had persuaded him to go to France. Bazargan appointed Yazdi to his cabinet and, in April 1979, Yazdi became foreign minister.

From early on Bazargan and his government faced two serious problems in running the state. In addition to Bazargan's government, new institutions were set up on Khomeini's orders. These included the Revolutionary Committees, or *komitehs* as they were called, and also the Revolutionary Council. The Council, whose existence was kept a secret until 1980, was known to be dominated by the ulama close to Khomeini, including former students Morteza Motahari, Muhammad Bahonar, and Muhammad Beheshti.

The Revolutionary Committees were local bodies set up throughout Iran whose purpose was to keep the revolution on what the radical ulama considered the right track. With Khomeini's encouragement the komitehs carried out hundreds of executions of perceived enemies of the revolution, including Amir Abbas Hoveyda, a former prime minister.

Khomeini and his supporters viewed these executions as a necessary part of the revolution. They saw victims of the purges as enemies of Islam and the revolution. These actions were criticized by Bazargan and other liberals, who saw this indifference to legal procedures as a dangerous precedent.

Bazargan, as well as the revolutionary movement itself, faced another problem: conflicting opinions about what the nature of the new state should be. Khomeini had made it clear that only an Islamic government was acceptable. However, few of the revolutionary groups could agree on what such a government was. Khomeini himself had left the question unanswered. His view was that the law of the state was contained in the Koran and Sunnah, and that this law could only be interpreted and applied by the highest-ranking ulama. Khomeini's comments concentrated on the importance of Islamic law for the new state and on the wide-ranging powers to be given to the person or persons running this state. Khomeini said little or nothing about political parties, a legislative branch, or any other democratic elements of government.

Two major conflicts arose between Bazargan and Khomeini's radical supporters. On March 31, 1979, a national referendum was held on the question of whether the Iranian people wanted an Islamic republic. Bazargan, along with both Ayatollah Taleqani and Ayatollah Shariatmadari, wanted a range of several types of government for the people to choose among. Khomeini and the radical ulama won out. The people were given only two choices: monarchy or an Islamic republic. The referendum was protested by the National Front, leftist political groups, and leading religious figures, including Shariatmadari. Large minorities such as Kurds, Turkomans, and others boycotted the referendum.

The first constitution of the new Islamic Republic was drawn up in June 1979. At the insistence of the radical ulama a second version was published in November 1979 and was approved by the Assembly of Experts, the new revolutionary legislative body that had been set up after Khomeini's return to Iran.

Under the new constitution the Islamic state's leadership was entrusted to a supreme "guide" from the ulama, the faqih. This figure was invested with extensive powers. Based directly upon Khomeini's doctrine of *velayet-e faqih* (governance of the jurist), Khomeini himself would occupy this position until his death. Historian Emmanuel Sivan notes that it was "only natural for him to think that the revolution (and the postrevolutionary government) must be controlled by himself as the Great Faqih of the Age and Vicar of the Hidden Imam."

> *Am I to resort to suppression, like the Shah? Our people have been in prison for 35 years; no government is going to put them in prison again. They must be given a chance to express themselves as they wish, even if it means a certain degree of chaos.*
> —AYATOLLAH KHOMEINI

Ayatollah Muhammad Beheshti discusses with the press the fate of the 53 Americans held hostage in Iran. Beheshti was one of the ulama close to Khomeini during his exile. Morteza Motahari, Muhammad Bahonar, and Beheshti were members of the Revolutionary Council, which controlled the new government from behind the scenes.

Schoolchildren carry a portrait of Ayatollah Kazem Shariatmadari in Tabriz, Iran. Shariatmadari rejected the 1979 constitution of the Islamic Republic that gave Khomeini final decision-making power as Iran's supreme legal guide, or faqih.

Bazargan, Yazdi, Ayatollah Shariatmadari and others immediately protested the constitution. Bazargan believed that a situation in which power was concentrated in the hands of one man was too close to what existed under the Shah. For Shariatmadari there was another problem. He complained that the doctrine of velayet-e faqih had not been indisputably established as part of Shi'ite law, and so should not form the basis of the constitution. The constitution allowed for such democratic elements as a cabinet and an elected parliament, but these were made secondary to the power of the faqih. Despite the objections of both Bazargan and Shariatmadari the new constitution was pushed through.

A political party called the Islamic Republican party (IRP) was formed by the radical ulama in 1979. The man who emerged as the head of the IRP was Ayatollah Muhammad Beheshti. A student of Khomeini in Najaf, Beheshti later served as a crucial link in the network that supported Khomeini within Iran during the latter's years in exile. For many ulama, Beheshti was an attractive choice as Khomeini's successor.

The IRP now controlled the Revolutionary Council, the Revolutionary Committees, a network of mosques, and the Revolutionary Guards, the new militia established after the revolution. In this way, the radical mullahs frustrated decisions by the Bazargan government.

The Iranian hostage crisis occurred when the revolution was still in its first stages. In Tehran and throughout Iran, a series of complex social, economic, and political problems had developed. As a result, the new government under Khomeini felt vulnerable. One fear was that the United States would take advantage of the situation to restore the Shah to power. These fears were seemingly confirmed by the American rescue attempt in April 1980 and by the presence of the Shah in the United States. By keeping its intentions toward the hostages vague, the new government hoped to make the United States ponder carefully any further military action.

Khomeini made use of the crisis to act against other groups of the revolution now in opposition to him. One tool in this conflict were the documents the diplomats at the U.S. Embassy tried to destroy. These documents contained information on groups the U.S. government thought it could count on for support. The radicals pieced the shredded papers together and published them. With the evidence the documents contained the radicals discredited these other groups through their connections to the Americans.

Bazargan and Yazdi were the first to fall victim to the crisis. Both Western-educated men who had shown a willingness to negotiate with the United States to end the hostage crisis, they quickly became the target of radical demonstrators. Left with no choice but to step down, Bazargan and Yazdi resigned on November 6, 1979. The Revolutionary Council immediately took over the government. Ayatollah Beheshti, as the secretary of the council, became, in effect, the new prime minister.

The IRP and the Revolutionary Committees by now were determining the course of events in Iran, with Khomeini's support. The revolutionary courts met regularly and continued to try alleged enemies of the revolution. The Revolutionary Guards, a group originally formed by Khomeini's supporters when the loyalties of the regular army were still in question, were growing stronger and adding to Khomeini's strength.

Finally, at the neighborhood level, groups of local toughs, called *hizbollahis*, or the groups of the Party of God, were growing in strength. They were aligned with local ulama, who used them to carry out measures deemed necessary for the revolution . Among these measures was one that forced women to wear veils in public. Women found unveiled were often harassed.

On January 25, 1980, in the midst of this struggle, a presidential election was held. Khomeini decided the ulama should concentrate on guiding the revolution and forbade them to run in the elections. This was a setback for Beheshti and the IRP, but their overall power remained undiminished; after the elections, they challenged the new president.

The president was Abolhasan Bani Sadr, a key participant in the revolution — and, eventually, an enemy of Khomeini. Like Bazargan and Yazdi, Bani

AP/WIDE WORLD

Women wearing the traditional black chadors leave a mosque in Tehran. When the Iranian revolution brought the radical ulama to power, their *komitehs* (Revolutionary Committees) began to enforce the *Sunnah* — Islam's "sacred customs." Women were required to wear traditional garb; those who did not conform were harassed.

Abolhasan Bani Sadr succeeded Bazargan as president in elections in February 1980. Though he initially had Khomeini's support, Bani Sadr was opposed by Beheshti's Islamic Republican party, who considered the president too liberal. He was driven from power in 1981 during the hostage crisis and took refuge in France.

UPI/BETTMANN NEWSPHOTOS

Sadr received part of his education in the West. Like them, he was convinced that the only acceptable form of government in Iran was one based on modern Islamic principles.

Before the revolution, Bani Sadr, Yazdi, and a man named Sadeq Qotbzadeh were Khomeini's principal lay (or nonclerical) advisers in France. Qotbzadeh had worked with Abolhasan Bani Sadr for some time in France against the Shah, and would become foreign minister under Bani Sadr. Both men, especially Bani Sadr, were close to Khomeini in 1979. Thus, when Bani Sadr won the presidency in February 1980 with 75 percent of the vote, he seemed to be in a position of strength. He was a popular figure and he enjoyed Khomeini's support. Yet the radical ulama disapproved of Bani Sadr and Qotbzadeh.

The IRP, and Beheshti in particular, led the struggle against Bani Sadr. Bani Sadr had the initial backing of Khomeini, as well as the middle class, many liberal and leftist groups, the army, and urban women, all of whom feared domination by the ulama. Nevertheless, the IRP dominated all the large revolutionary organizations. The IRP also controlled the National Assembly. As a result, Beheshti blocked most of Bani Sadr's political initiatives.

At first Khomeini tried to bring the two groups together. Failing to do so, Khomeini grew insistent on unity of opinion within the revolution. He grew uncomfortable with Bani Sadr's more Western-influenced ideas, and critical of Bani Sadr's handling of the government. Bani Sadr struggled for months with the daily problems of governing but was consistently frustrated by the IRP. Always sensitive to political currents, Khomeini was aware of the growing power of the IRP and Beheshti. Finally, he decided to back the IRP in its conflict with Bani Sadr.

That Bani Sadr could be critical and often even insulting in his statements did not help his position. Opposition to him grew vocal and more violent. One weapon used against him was the hostage crisis. Once in office, Bani Sadr declared the embassy takeover unwise and responsible for unnecessary diplomatic problems for Iran. He and Qotbzadeh struggled for months to resolve the crisis and have the hostages released. Negotiations with the United States seemed unavoidable. This the radicals rejected. As Bani Sadr continued to address the issue, his adversaries turned it against him.

In June 1981 the National Assembly, dominated by the radicals, voted to impeach Bani Sadr. His followers were arrested, and Bani Sadr went underground. In July he fled Iran. He went to France and, along with several other figures, formed a political group whose stated aim was the overthrow of Khomeini. The hostage crisis was not the only factor in Bani Sadr's downfall but it was an important one.

The fall of Bani Sadr was a victory for Beheshti and the IRP, and was an important step in the consolidation of their power. In the late months of 1980 and throughout 1981, a series of violent battles were fought in the streets of Tehran and other cities between the Revolutionary Guards and the leftist Mojahedin. The Guards and the IRP emerged victorious in this fight, but at the cost of their top leadership, including Beheshti.

Like the National Front, the leftist guerrillas supported Khomeini as the head of the revolution, although they did not agree with all his ideas. For Khomeini, these groups had proved helpful in organizing demonstrations, and in the fighting of 1978–1979 against the Shah's troops. At the same time, he distrusted their ideas, so different from his own, which he saw as strongly Western in character. He was wary of the military experience they had gained in fighting the Shah. Soon after returning to Iran, Khomeini began accusing them of fomenting unrest. He and the IRP also blocked any leftist participation in the government.

On June 28, 1981, the angered leftists set off a bomb at the headquarters of the IRP, killing Beheshti and a number of other party officials. On August 30 another explosion killed the new president, Muhammad Ali Raja'i, and the new prime minister, Muhammad Javad Bahonar. Several other assassinations followed.

The government was severely shaken by these deaths. However, on Khomeini's urging, ruthless retaliatory measures were taken. Mass arrests and executions, especially of Mojahedin members, were

Islam is the first school of social thought that recognizes the masses as the basis, the fundamental and conscious factor in determining history and society.
—ALI SHARIATI
Iranian sociologist

Sadeq Qotbzadeh addresses a rally in 1978. Qotbzadeh, Yazdi, and Bani Sadr had all been close advisers to Khomeini, although they were not members of the ulama. Qotbzadeh became foreign minister under Bani Sadr's presidency, but he was accused of plotting against the state and executed in 1982.

AP/WIDE WORLD

carried out. Vicious street battles raged for months. Between these and the executions, believed to number over 2,500, the leftists suffered terrible losses. By the end of 1981 the Feda'iyan-e and other smaller groups were permanently crippled. The Mojahedin survived and continued its activities, but it was badly weakened and could no longer pose a challenge to the state. Within two years the Tudeh party — which had backed Khomeini from the start of the revolution — had also been crippled by bans and arrests. The campaign against the leftists was a further step taken by Khomeini and the IRP to control political forces in Iran.

Some of the ulama were alarmed by Khomeini's ideas and the radicalism of his followers. After Ayatollah Taleqani died in 1979, the only religious figure to pose any threat to the state was Ayatollah Shariatmadari. His relationship with Khomeini had been strained even before the revolution. In 1979 he formed the Islamic People's Republican party to counter the power of the IRP. This party gathered support, but Khomeini had it disbanded and outlawed. Several of its leaders were executed; Shariatmadari was discredited. In April 1982 Khomeini again moved against his fellow ayatollah. It was announced that a plot against the state had been uncovered. Qotbzadeh, the former foreign minister, and Shariatmadari were accused of organizing the plot. Qotbzadeh was tried and executed, and Shariatmadari was placed under house arrest until his death in April 1986.

Khomeini's behavior during the struggle for control again showed his political abilities. Time and again he correctly interpreted political developments. He strengthened his own position even when conflicts were raging around him. He at first encouraged groups such as the National Front and the Tudeh to cooperate with him in his struggle against the Shah, but after the revolution, when their support was no longer desirable, he again stressed his doctrine of the Great Faqih.

Most often, Khomeini stayed aloof from numerous specific political and economic problems. He was inclined towards more general, theoretical issues rather than the practical concerns of government.

CALL TO RISE UP AGAINST OPPRESSION

Imam Khomeini's Christmas Message
to The Christian World

Imam Khomeini gave his Christmas message to the Christians of the world on December 24, 1979. To have it reach you on Christmas Day we planned to print it in the WASHINGTON POST. But the Post refused the message unless we changed some words. Since these are the exact words of the Imam, we could not change them. Therefore, this message, meant for the holy day of Christmas itself, is reaching you after Christmas.

In the Name of God, the Compassionate, the Merciful

O Believers, rise up and be steadfast witnesses for God in equity and justice, and do not let hatred of any people turn you away from justice. Deal justly, that is nearer to righteousness. Observe your duty to God. For God knows what you do.
Holy Quran, Sura Ma'idah, aya 8

Blessed are those who hunger and thirst after justice for they shall be filled.
Matthew, Chapter 5, verse 6

Blessed are those who are persecuted for justice sake: for theirs is the kingdom of Heaven.
Matthew, Chapter 5, verse 10

Merry Christmas to the oppressed nations of the world, to the Christian nations and the Christians of Iran. Christ was a great messenger whose mission was to establish justice and mercy, and who with his heavenly words and deeds condemned the tyrants and supported the oppressed.

You priests and clergy, followers of Christ, rise up and give your support to the oppressed of the world against the oppressors, and for the sake of God and the teachings of Jesus Christ, ring the bells of your churches just once in support of the oppressed of Iran and in condemnation of the oppressors.

Carter, vanguard of the world's oppressors, called for the bells to be rung throughout the United States in support of his agents against the deprived Iranian nation. How good and appropriate that you ring the bells according to the order of God and the teachings of Jesus Christ in support of the oppressed nations crushed under the boots of Carter's soldiers.

Happy are those who are hungry and thirsty for justice and strive after it. Woe to those who strive against the teachings of Jesus Christ and all the prophets, for the sake of spies and oppressors of the rights of nations.

And O Nation of the Messiah, and followers of Jesus, the spirit of God, rise up and defend the dignity of Jesus Christ, and the nation of Christianity, and do not let the enemies of the divine teachings and the opposers of godly orders give false impression of Christianity and its clergy to the oppressed peoples of the world. Do not be deceived by the presence of the super powers in churches, or by their prayers for spies and traitors. They think of nothing but more power, or supremacy over the world, which is against divine teachings. Our nation suffered from the hypocrisy of the oppressors for many years.

O Christians, what happened that Mr. Carter did not rise up against the massacres in Iran, Vietnam, Palestine, Lebanon and elsewhere, and did not request the ringing of the bells? But now he has begun to pray, and has called upon the churches to ring the bells, for another term as President and for a few more years' continued suppression of the weakened nations.

O fathers of the church, rise up and save Jesus Christ from the clutches of these executioners, since that great prophet dislikes the oppressor who uses religion as a tool of tyranny and prayer as a tool for reaching the throne of oppression over the creatures of God, since the heavenly teachings were sent down to release the oppressed.

And you, the oppressed of the world, arise and unite to be rid of the oppressors, for the earth belongs to God, and its inheritors are the oppressed.

And you, the American nation, do not listen to the propaganda of Presidents who think of nothing but power, and be sure that our youth will treat the spies in a manner pleasing to God, because Islam orders us to have mercy on captives, even if they are tyrants and spies.

You the American nation, ask Carter to return the criminal deposed Shah to Iran because the key to the release of the spies is in his hands.

And you who ring the bells, pray and ring the bells and beg God Almighty to confer a sense of justice and fairness on your presidents.

Happy are those who strive after justice and pray.

EMBASSY OF THE ISLAMIC REPUBLIC OF IRAN

WASHINGTON, D.C.—CHRISTMAS 1979

The U.S. newspaper *Washington Post* refused to print this "Christmas Message" from Khomeini, addressing Christians on Christmas 1979, after the U.S. Embassy and 53 hostages were seized in Tehran. Khomeini told the American people "to ask (President) Carter to return the criminal deposed Shah," then in the United States.

Khomeini, accompanied by his son Ahmed, casts his ballot in Iran's parliamentary elections after the 1979 revolution. In March 1979 Khomeini and Bazargan clashed when the Iranian people were asked to choose either a monarchy or an Islamic government.

Khomeini had little formal knowledge of economics and administration, thus he could not be expected to answer questions concerning them.

Khomeini took an active role in legal and religious affairs and in fighting against the opposition. He attached great importance to the unification and spread of Islam. He watched over the then developing Islamic court system and legal codes, paying close attention to legislation and the appointment of judges and other officials. He had seen the Shah fail to solve certain problems and noted how this had contributed to his downfall. Khomeini left controversial and unpopular issues for others to solve, and this helped him maintain his position.

By the end of 1982 the revolutionary regime was stronger than ever. The militant factions among Khomeini's followers carried out numerous arrests and executions. They purged universities and other institutions. Through 1982 and 1983, during a severe repressive crackdown, perhaps as many as 10,000 people were executed; the number of political prisoners may have reached 40,000.

More than one opinion is expressed on this roadside "editorial" to American drivers during the hostage crisis. The United States was still adjusting to the sudden increases in world oil prices, which soared in 1974. The 444-day hostage crisis deepened American anger toward Khomeini and Iran.

Fight back... **Drive 55!** FIGHT EXXON - NOT IRAN A BILLBOARD EDITORIAL

More often than not, innocent people were victims of these activities. The stated rationale for these campaigns was the "Islamization" of Iranian society. Arbitrary and violent behavior by the radicals and the Revolutionary Guards only worsened tensions and lessened support for the state and for Khomeini himself.

Skilled and educated Iranians began leaving the country, which disrupted the economy. Finally, in December 1982, Khomeini issued an eight-point declaration condemning the revolutionary excesses and banning certain activities. The Revolutionary Guards and the courts were told to act with greater moderation. Aware that support for the revolution was dwindling because of the extensive use of terror, Khomeini made more than a dozen speeches in which he stressed that the period of revolutionary activity was over. The time had come for new stability, he said.

The result was noticeable. Campaigns of violence by the Guards and radical ulama came to a stop. It was clear that Khomeini and the revolutionary institutions were now firmly in place. They had suppressed the opposition and were now in a position to deal with other problems that had developed over the past few years.

The former Shah of Iran, ill with cancer, and Egypt's President Anwar el-Sadat arrive at the Maadi Military Hospital in Cairo, Egypt. After his presence in the United States sparked the seizure of the U.S. Embassy in Tehran and further Iranian demands that he be handed back, the Shah took up residence in Egypt. He died there in 1980.

101

9

Martyrs

Khomeini and the revolutionary organizations emerged firmly in control of the Islamic Republic by the end of 1982. However, the new revolutionary state still faced severe difficulties. First there was the Iranian economy, which lay in shambles in the aftermath of the Shah's fall and the power struggles that marked the early days of the Islamic Republic. Land reform, the nationalization of banks and the oil industry, and other economic measures were carried out chaotically. But the state of the economy had already become secondary to a far more urgent matter — war.

On September 22, 1980, after several months of small skirmishes over a border dispute, Iraqi aircraft bombed a number of locations in Iran while Iraqi troops stormed across the border in the south. The Persian Gulf War, which would claim more than 1 million lives over the next eight years, had begun.

Saddam Hussein, the Iraqi president, had other reasons besides the border dispute to wage war on Iran. Wary of the spread of the Iranian Revolution,

> *Islam was dead or dying for nearly fourteen centuries; we have revived it with the blood of our youth. . . . We shall soon liberate Jerusalem and pray there.*
> —AYATOLLAH KHOMEINI

Dead Iraqi troops after an Iranian attack in the Persian Gulf War (1980–88). Khomeini pronounced the conflict, which claimed more than 1 million lives, a holy war. But the zeal of the Iranian people disappeared after years of stalemate that ruined the economy and left millions of Iran's young men dead or crippled.

REUTERS/BETTMANN NEWSPHOTOS

he sought to smash the new Iranian government while also securing a more strategic position over the Persian Gulf, and possibly seizing Iran's oil fields. He also hoped to become a dominant power among the Arab nations. Finally there was the age-old enmity between the Arab Iraqis and the Persian Iranians; the two nations had skirmished for decades over ownership of the Shatt-al-Arab waterway at the oil-rich north end of the Persian Gulf, but the dispute had always contained more than a little ethnic and religious hatred.

At first the war was a disaster for Iran. The revolution had damaged the strength of the armed forces and lowered the credibility of the officer corps in particular. Arms supplies were low, many officers were purged, and most units of the army were only barely functional. Iraqi troops captured Iran's largest ports, Abadan and Khorramshahr. Iraqi planes destroyed 65 percent of Iran's oil refineries and struck many towns and cities in western Iran, causing many Iranians to become refugees. Costs to Iran of this initial period of the war were extremely high.

Finally, the Iranian army, with the help of volunteers and the Revolutionary Guards, assembled enough men and artillery to repel the attack. Meanwhile, the government scrambled to rebuild the armed forces. Over the next year, the

Khomeini meets with Yasser Arafat, the leader of the Palestine Liberation Organization (PLO), in Tehran in 1979. Arafat's group, which uses both diplomatic and violent means in its struggle to create an independent state for Palestinians, trained more than 10,000 guerrillas specifically for Iran's Islamic government. Also pictured are Khomeini's son Ahmed and "Judge Blood" Khalkali.

officer corps regained unity and confidence; more arms were purchased. The war helped to increase the strength and organization of the Revolutionary Guards. As a result, the conflict between Iran and Iraq turned into a long war of attrition.

By the end of 1981 Iranian forces had recaptured Khorramshahr and pushed the Iraqis back on the defensive. Khomeini's decision to invade Iraq came on June 21, 1982. He issued a statement calling for the overthrow of President Saddam Hussein. Khomeini sensed the opportunity had come to "export" the revolution. He also saw a chance to avenge the initial Iraqi onslaught. With Hussein's overthrow, he stated, the Iraqi people would unite with Iran. Smaller states in the region would, in turn, undergo a similar process and submit to Khomeini's leadership. Khomeini's efforts to spread the revolution were not limited to Iraq. He and his followers also focused on other areas, particularly those with Shi'a communities — the Persian Gulf States (Bahrain, Qatar, and the United Arab Emirates) and Lebanon.

Despite efforts by several nations to end the conflict, Khomeini insisted on the need to overthrow Hussein: "The Islamic government of Iran cannot sit at the peace table with a government that has no faith in Islam and in humanity. Islam does not allow peace between us and him, between a Muslim and an infidel." To undermine the Iraqi government, Khomeini helped form an Iraqi opposition movement based in Tehran, and encouraged the large Shi'ite population in Iraq to undermine Hussein. The Iraqi Shi'ites' response was limited, however, partly because of Hussein's efforts to control all activity among them.

Khomeini frequently spoke of Islam as a weapon with which to defeat tyrants and hostile foreign powers, such as the United States and Israel. Officials of Khomeini's government asserted that Khomeini, as the faqih, was the rightful leader of all the Shi'a and, indeed, of Muslims everywhere.

In 1982 Khomeini sent a group led by Mohammed Khoeiniha on the hajj, the Islamic spiritual pilgrimage to Mecca, in Saudi Arabia. The Iranian radicals, waving pictures of Khomeini and chanting slogans, clashed with Saudi Arabian police. In 1982 and

Hovering like some immense yet scarcely visible monster over much of the most dramatic news of the past decade, including not only Iran but the Arab-Israeli conflict, oil, and Afghanistan, has been "Islam."
—EDWARD SAID

1983 Khomeini attacked the Saudi Arabian government as unfit to oversee the hajj. He urged Iranian pilgrims to "use the hajj for an Islamic uprising." In 1987 a riot broke out during the hajj between Iranian and anti-Iranian pilgrims. Saudi police, firing live ammunition, intervened, killing more than 400 Iranians. The next year Saudi Arabia broke off diplomatic relations with Iran.

Khomeini's followers were also active in Lebanon. Iran sent a contingent of Revolutionary Guards to Lebanon to help counter the Israeli invasion of that country in the summer of 1982. Khomeini directed many statements to the large Lebanese Shi'ite population. Iran was also accused of having organized the bombing of the U.S. Embassy in Beirut in April 1982 as well as the car-bomb attacks in October 1983 against American, French, and Israeli barracks that resulted in more than 300 deaths.

Through the mid-1980s, Khomeini used his power as head of state to appoint top judges and the commanders of the armed forces. He frequently sent personal representatives to various regions of the country to settle disputes and supervise local jurisdictions. In control of the central government, he increased the power of the ulama, and by the middle of the decade nearly all the top government ministers were clerics.

But the war with Iraq remained Iran's overriding concern. With Iran's air force grounded for lack of spare parts and trained pilots, Iraqi planes conducted daily bombing raids on Iranian targets while both sides fired long-range missiles at each other's cities. Meanwhile, on the ground, the Iraqis dug in along the border and were content to wage trench warfare; the Iranians, urged on by Khomeini's call for total victory, were cut down by the thousands in futile "human wave" assaults on the well-fortified Iraqi positions. The victims in these assaults were usually teenage Revolutionary Guards, who eagerly volunteered for what they believed was martyrdom in the war against the Iraqis; some entered battle clad in white, the traditional Iranian color of death and mourning. Cemeteries throughout Iran were crowded to overflowing with the graves of soldiers and civilians killed in the war, and weekend family visits to the grave sites of fallen loved ones became a common practice. The celebration of martyrdom, always a principal feature of Shi'ism, reached new levels as a result of the war; the water in the main fountain at Bahesht-e-Zahra, Tehran's largest cemetery, was dyed red to make it look like blood.

Fearful that the better-equipped Iraqi military would prevail, Khomeini approved secret efforts by Iran to obtain arms from foreign governments, primarily Israel — a particularly ironic choice in light of Khomeini's relentless anti-Israeli rhetoric. Clandestine Israeli munitions shipments solved the arms shortage for a while, but soon Iran was seeking more arms from an even less likely source: the United States.

Certain figures in the Iranian government hinted to the Reagan administration that, in exchange for secret arms shipments, Iran would arrange the release of fewer than a dozen Americans held hostage by Shi'ite militias in Lebanon. In 1985, Lieutenant

In 1983 a series of car-bomb attacks were launched against American, French, and Israeli barracks in Beirut, Lebanon, allegedly by followers of Khomeini. Here U.S. Marines carry a dead comrade from the rubble in October of that year, in the aftermath of a bombing that killed 241 marines.

A group of chanting Iranian soldiers after a 1984 attack on an Iraqi oil refinery in the Majnoon Islands. With weapons supplies running low in the mid-1980s, Iran made secret deals to buy arms from Israel. Another secret deal, with the United States, violated U.S. law, giving rise to a scandal that led to the resignation of three top officials in the Reagan administration.

Colonel Oliver North, a U.S. Marine officer assigned to the White House staff, carried out the deal on the orders of his superiors. North then took the profits from the secret arms sales and used them to purchase weapons and equipment for a group of rebels trying to overthrow the Nicaraguan government. Several top officials in the U.S. government were involved, and there is some evidence that President Reagan and Vice-President George Bush approved the deal. It was an enormously complex operation, and, according to the U.S. Congress and American courts, one that violated U.S. laws. When the deal was uncovered by government investigators and the international press, it caused enormous embarrassment to the Reagan administration. The United States had been caught trading arms for hostages with a so-called terrorist nation, something Reagan

had repeatedly vowed that the U.S. government would never do.

In the end, the missiles and other munitions Iran received from the United States and other nations enabled it to keep the war stalemated; the Shi'ite militias in Lebanon released only some of the American hostages; and the Reagan administration, which had hoped the secret arms sales would somehow lead to the weakening or even the overthrow of Khomeini, found that the Ayatollah emerged from the affair as strong as ever. Khomeini, who had helped cause the downfall of President Carter, had now greatly damaged the presidency of Ronald Reagan as well.

Khomeini deflected any potential domestic criticism of Iran's dealings with "the Great Satan" by blaming the officials in the Iranian government who dealt directly with the United States. "I never expected such things from such people," he claimed. It was a tactic Khomeini had used before whenever a plan or initiative had proven embarrassing. He was expert at distancing himself from an official, program, or principle at just the right moment. As Shaul Bakhash, an Iranian historian living in the United States, wrote in the *New York Review of Books* in July 1989, Khomeini, "to maintain power, to preserve the Islamic republic he had founded, [was] capable of setting aside his 'principles' and of both tactical and large-scale retreats." Khomeini, wrote Bakhash, "gave up the American hostages, although none of the conditions he had insisted on for 14 months were met. . . . He called for the elimination of Israel, but bought arms from the Israelis. He branded America the Great Satan, but agreed to trade arms for hostages and to permit an Iranian emissary to negotiate in the White House with Oliver North. . . . He repeatedly denounced the rich and the privileged; yet he gave no support to radical measures for wealth distribution. . . . He endorsed a radical program for redistributing land; then, when clerical opposition grew and disorder spread in the countryside, he abandoned the land reform. . . . Repeatedly, he endorsed the resumption of normal relations with the West; repeatedly he personally

Ayatollah Husayn Ali Montazeri speaks at a prayer meeting at Tehran University on November 30, 1979. Montazeri, who until March 1989 was Khomeini's designated successor, tried to reopen relations with the West. But Khomeini dismissed him after he criticized a series of executions in 1988 and 1989.

undermined such initiatives or stood by as radicals in the leadership did so with impunity."

The Iran-Iraq war dragged on into its seventh year in 1987. In July, after the collapse of the arms-for-hostages deal, U.S. Navy warships entered the Persian Gulf to escort Kuwaiti oil tankers to refineries near the battle zone. Iranian boats and gun platforms exchanged fire with far more powerful American ships and aircraft on several occasions, usually suffering much heavier losses than they inflicted.

At the front itself Iran's army was being worn down by the well-entrenched Iraqi forces, who used poison gas to inflict enormous casualties on Iranian troops. Iran could no longer sustain the cost of the seemingly endless war, and toward the end of the year it launched a desperate all-or-nothing offensive to try to push the Iraqis back one last time. After some initial Iranian gains, the Iraqis counterattacked, threw the Iranian army back, and crossed into Iran. Another blow fell on July 3, 1988, when an American warship accidentally shot down an Iranian passenger jet, killing all 290 people aboard.

Fifteen days later, Iran accepted a UN cease-fire plan. Some of the leading figures in the Iranian government—including President Hojatolislam Ali Khamenei, speaker of the parliament Ali Akbar Hashemi Rafsanjani, and Khomeini's designated successor, Ayatollah Husayn Ali Montazeri—had finally succeeded in convincing Khomeini to accept a truce."I had promised to fight to the last drop of my blood and to my last breath," Khomeini told the nation in a radio address. "Taking this decision was more deadly than swallowing poison. I submitted myself to God's will and drank this drink for his satisfaction." On August 20, 1988, the cease-fire went into effect. The Persian Gulf War was over.

Khamenei, Rafsanjani, and Montazeri had already been working quietly to reopen relations with several European governments in the hope of attracting investment—the only way, they believed, for Iran to rebuild its war-shattered economy. By the beginning of 1989, their efforts, which Khomeini had apparently approved, were showing signs of success.

At the same time, however, a controversial novel, *The Satanic Verses*, was published in Britain. Written by the prominent Pakistani-born British author Salman Rushdie (who was raised a Muslim but who had since renounced the religion), the novel portrayed a character based on Khomeini in an unflattering light. Another character, based on the prophet Muhammad, was also portrayed unflatteringly in the novel. Muslims throughout the world were outraged; they believed the novel blasphemed Islam.

Then, in February 1989, Khomeini spoke out against Rushdie. "The author of the 'Satanic Verses' book," said the Ayatollah, "which is against Islam, the Prophet, and the Koran, and all those involved in its publication who were aware of its content, are sentenced to death." Faced with the threat against his life, Rushdie went into hiding; bookstores across Europe and North America pulled the novel off their shelves. Incensed Western governments

Tehran students denounce British author Salman Rushdie's novel *The Satanic Verses*, which enraged Muslims throughout the world for its allegedly blasphemous depiction of the prophet Muhammad. In February 1989 Khomeini called for Rushdie's "execution," prompting outraged Western governments to withdraw offers of economic aid to Iran.

A moderate influence on the radical Khomeini, Ali Akbar Hashemi Rafsanjani, speaker of the parliament, helped convince the Ayatollah to accept a cease-fire in the Iran-Iraq war in August 1988. After Khomeini's death, Rafsanjani was named Iran's head of state.

broke off relations with Iran, wrecking the efforts of Khamenei, Rafsanjani, and Montazeri to reestablish ties with Europe. Indeed, many observers believed that the real reason the Ayatollah threatened Rushdie's life was to short-circuit those efforts.

Although the Rushdie affair captured the world's attention, a more tangible and widespread form of violence was taking place within Iran itself. In the 6 months that followed the cease-fire with Iraq, a new round of executions in Iran claimed the lives of more than 1,000 political prisoners and members of the opposition (a large number, but not as large as the 7,000 former officials of the Shah, SAVAK torturers, drug dealers, prostitutes, adulterers, homosexuals, and members of minority religious groups who were executed immediately after the 1979 revolution). Rafsanjani apparently approved of the 1988–89 executions, but Montazeri did not and sharply advised Khomeini to stop them. In March 1989, Montazeri spoke out publicly against the executions and, belatedly, against the war with

Iraq. Khomeini responded by denouncing him; shortly thereafter the Ayatollah told the nation that Montazeri was no longer his designated successor. Thus Khomeini, old and in ill health, created yet another crisis: No one knew who would succeed him as faqih.

Three months later, at three o'clock on the afternoon of June 3, 1989, Khomeini suffered a heart attack. Doctors revived him, according to Iranian newspapers, and "he whispered prayers," although he was unable to speak to relatives and officials who gathered by his bedside. "As the night moved closer," reported the Iranian newspaper *Resalat,* "the Imam slid further into silence and, finally, at about midnight, the long spirit of God joined celestial heaven." Ayatollah Ruhollah Khomeini was dead.

Hundreds of thousands of grieving Iranians poured into the streets of Tehran and other cities when they heard the news of Khomeini's death. Throngs of weeping men and women beat their chests and heads in a traditional Iranian display of grief. "We have been orphaned," cried one distraught woman; "our father is dead."

After Khomeini's death Hojatolislam Ali Khamenei, one of the key moderates in the Iranian government, was named Iran's supreme religious leader, winning out over Khomeini's son Ahmed.

In 1982, Khomeini had deposited a sealed political testament in a safe, to be opened upon his death. Now an 83-member board of theological experts opened the 29-page document to see what provisions Khomeini would recommend for the future. The document was read over Tehran radio. The king of Saudi Arabia was "a traitor to God," according to Khomeini's will. Iraq's Saddam Hussein and the leaders of Jordan, Morocco, and the United States were "terrorists" and "pirates," said the document. "May God's curse be upon them." But Khomeini left no recommendations for conducting the affairs of government. It was up to the theological experts to choose Khomeini's successor. Would it be the hardliner Ahmed Khomeini, the late Imam's son, or Ali Khamenei, the relatively moderate president of the Islamic Republic? The experts chose Khamenei, but it remained to be seen how much power he would actually have in post-Khomeini Iran.

There was to be one last spectacular episode involving Ruhollah Khomeini, the man who had forged and led the Islamic Revolution, one of the most significant mass movements of the 20th century.

On June 6, Khomeini's body, lying in a refrigerated glass case, was placed on a makeshift platform of cargo containers in Bahesht-e-Zahra cemetery in Tehran. Three million grieving Iranians surrounded the case to mourn their leader — a crowd even larger than the one that greeted Khomeini on his return to Iran 10 years before. The mourners moved in a titanic crush to get closer to his body, and at least eight people were trampled to death. Fire hoses sprayed the crowd with cool water on the intensely hot day, but scores of people fainted nevertheless and had to be passed over the heads of the throng to waiting ambulances. Officials who wished to pay their respects hovered just over the coffin in helicopters; it was the only way they could get close. "Sorrow, sorrow is this day, Khomeini the idol-smasher is with God today," chanted the millions of mourners. "We have lost our father! This nation, what will it do without you?"

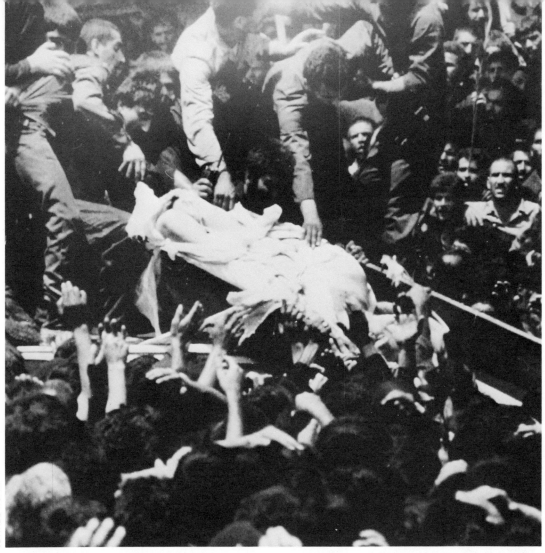

People flung themselves into the Ayatollah's waiting grave as a helicopter tried to pick up the body and move it to the grave site. But the mourners pulled the bier off the helicopter and held the coffin aloft. Khomeini's body tumbled out, and hundreds of people grabbed at it, trying to tear pieces from the burial shroud as sacred relics. The burial detail, firing gunshots into the air to scatter the crowd, finally retrieved the corpse.

It took five hours to clear the area sufficiently to proceed with the burial, which was broadcast live on state television. The newsreader narrating the coverage broke down in tears when Khomeini's body was lowered into the grave. "O martyr!" he cried.

Khomeini's corpse tumbles from its casket as frenzied mourners tear at its shroud during the Ayatollah's funeral on June 6, 1989. Despite the huge outpouring of grief — of the 3 million people who attended the funeral, 8 were trampled to death and scores were injured — many of the strictures Khomeini had imposed on Iranian society were lifted soon after his death.

Further Reading

Afshar, Haleh, ed. *Iran: A Revolution in Turmoil.* London: Macmillan, 1985.

Albert, David H., ed. *Tell the American People: Perspectives on the Iranian Revolution.* Andalusia, PA: Hallowell & Wess, 1980.

Bakhash, Shaul. *Reign of the Ayatollahs: Iran & the Islamic Revolution.* New York: Basic Books, 1986.

Bill, James A. *The Eagle and the Lion: The Tragedy of American-Iranian Relations.* New Haven: Yale University Press, 1988.

Cockroft, James D. *Mohammed Reza Pahlavi, Shah of Iran.* New York: Chelsea House, 1988.

Cohen, William S., and George J. Mitchell. *Men of Zeal: A Candid Story of the Iran-Contra Hearings.* New York: Viking Press, 1988.

Graham, Robert. *Iran: The Illusion of Power.* London: Croom Helm, 1978.

Heikal, Mohamed. *Iran: The Untold Story.* New York: Pantheon Books, 1982.

Hoveyda, Fereydoun. *The Fall of the Shah.* New York: Wyndham Books, 1980.

Irving, Clive, ed. *Sayings of Ayatollah Khomeini.* New York: Bantam Books, 1980.

Laing, Margaret Irene. *The Shah.* London: Sidgwick and Jackson, 1977.

Mannetti, Lisa. *Iran and Iraq: Nations at War.* New York: Watts, 1986.

Mottahedeh, Roy P. *The Mantle of the Prophet: Religion and Politics in Iran.* New York: Simon & Schuster, 1985.

Rafizadeh, Mansur. *Witness: Secret Arms Scandal.* New York: Morrow, 1987.

Rosen, Barry M., ed. *Iran Since the Revolution: Internal Dynamics, Regional Conflict, and the Superpowers.* New York: Columbia University Press, 1985.

Rubin, Barry. *Paved with Good Intentions: The American Experiences in Iran.* New York: Penguin Books, 1981.

Simpson, John. *Inside Iran: Life Under Khomeini's Regime.* New York: St. Martin's Press, 1988.

Taheri, Amir. *The Spirit of Allah: Khomeini and the Islamic Revolution.* London: Hutchinson, 1985.

Wright, Robin. *Sacred Rage: The Wrath of Militant Islam.* New York: Touchstone, 1986.

Chronology

Nov. 1902 (?)	Born Ruhollah Khomeini in Khomein, Persia
1903	Khomeini's father is murdered
1919	Khomeini moves to Arak to study Islamic law and religion; moves to Qom in 1921
1925	Reza Shah comes to power, founding the Pahlavi dynasty
c. 1931	Khomeini begins teaching in the Faiziyeh school
1941	Reza Shah abdicates in favor of his son, Mohammed Reza Shah Pahlavi; Khomeini writes *The Unveiling of the Secrets*
April 1951	Muhammad Mossadeq becomes prime minister
1953	With American and British help, Mossadeq is ousted and Mohammed Reza Shah Pahlavi is returned to power
1963	Khomeini launches a campaign against the Shah's reforms
June 5, 1963	Arrested for accusing the Shah's regime of plotting to destroy Islam; riots ensue and martial law is declared
April 1964	Released from prison
Oct. 1964	Criticizes an Iranian law granting diplomatic immunity to U.S. military personnel; forced into exile in Turkey and later Iraq
Oct. 1977	Khomeini's son Mostafa dies under mysterious circumstances in Iraq
1978	A Tehran newspaper publishes an attack on Khomeini, sparking riots in which hundreds are killed; Khomeini is expelled from Iraq and goes to France
Jan. 16, 1979	Mohammed Reza Shah Pahlavi is driven from Iran
Jan. 31, 1979	Khomeini returns to Iran and becomes the national ruler
Nov. 4, 1979	Iranian students storm U.S. Embassy and hold the personnel hostage
Sept. 22, 1980	Iraq invades Iran, eight-year war between the two nations begins
Jan. 20, 1981	The American hostages are released
Oct. 1983	Iran accused of plotting car-bomb attacks that kill more than 300 U.S., French, and Israeli troops in Lebanon
1985	Secret arms deal between United States and Iran
July 1987	U.S. Navy enters Persian Gulf to escort Kuwaiti tankers, clashes with Iranian forces ensue
July 1988	U.S. warship accidentally shoots down Iranian passenger plane, killing 290; Khomeini accepts cease-fire with Iraq
Feb. 1989	Khomeini calls for death of British author Salman Rushdie
Mar. 1989	Dismisses designated successor, Husayn Ali Montazeri, after Montazeri denounces mass executions
June 1989	Khomeini dies (June 3); Hojatolislam Ali Khamenei named successor (June 4); Khomeini buried at Bahesht-e-Zahra cemetery in Tehran (June 6)

Index

Matthew S. Gordon was born in Princeton, New Jersey, and grew up in Beirut, Lebanon, where his parents taught at the American University of Beirut. He received his B.A. in European History from Drew University in 1979, and is currently enrolled in the graduate program for Middle East Studies at Columbia University. He expects to receive his doctorate in 1989.

Arthur M. Schlesinger, jr., taught history at Harvard for many years and is currently Albert Schweitzer Professor of the Humanities at City University of New York. He is the author of numerous highly praised works in American history and has twice been awarded the Pulitzer Prize. He served in the White House as special assistant to Presidents Kennedy and Johnson.

Matthew S. Gordon was born in Princeton, New Jersey, and grew up in Beirut, Lebanon, where his parents taught at the American University of Beirut. He received his B.A. in European History from Drew University in 1979, and is currently enrolled in the graduate program for Middle East Studies at Columbia University. He expects to receive his doctorate in 1989.

Arthur M. Schlesinger, jr., taught history at Harvard for many years and is currently Albert Schweitzer Professor of the Humanities at City University of New York. He is the author of numerous highly praised works in American history and has twice been awarded the Pulitzer Prize. He served in the White House as special assistant to Presidents Kennedy and Johnson.